A. Macpherson.

590

PUFFIN BOOKS

ANIMALS MATTER

In response to a Blue Peter competition on BBC TV in March 1991, over 41,000 viewers sent in articles, stories, recipes, poems, pictures and cartoons on the theme of animal conservation. We have chosen some of the best for *Animals Matter*. The authors of this book are aged between 4 and 15, all of whom watch Blue Peter, and all have shown how much they care about animals.

Topics chosen range from saving the elephants to making bird-cake; from vivisection to vegetarianism; from bats to bumble-bees; from frogs to hedgehogs. There's plenty for everyone to read and think about as well as puzzles to do, a badge to make and some delicious recipes to try out. And even if you did not enter the competition, just by buying this book you will be showing that YOU care, as all the royalties are going to the Royal Society for the Protection of Birds (RSPB).

D0994048

Animals Matter

Illustrated by Tony Ross

PUFFIN BOOKS

PUFFIN BOOKS

Published by the Penguin Group
Penguin Books Ltd, 27 Wrights Lane, London W8 5TZ, England
Penguin Books USA Inc., 375 Hudson Street, New York, New York 10014, USA
Penguin Books Australia Ltd, Ringwood, Victoria, Australia
Penguin Books Canada Ltd, 10 Alcorn Avenue, Toronto, Ontario, Canada M4V 3B2
Penguin Books (NZ) Ltd, 182–190 Wairau Road, Auckland 10, New Zealand

Penguin Books Ltd, Registered Offices: Harmondsworth, Middlesex, England

First published 1991
10 9 8 7 6 5 4 3 2 1

The views and facts expressed by the contributors in this book
are not necessarily those held by BBC Television or Penguin Books Ltd.

Printed in England by Clays Ltd, St Ives plc

CONTENTS

ALEX POSTLE   GWENT, SOUTH WALES

FOREWORD

Animals Matter has been a wonderful *Blue Peter* competition, a great celebration for Puffin Books, whose 50th birthday the competition marks, valuable for the RSPB, who will receive the royalties from this book, and – best of all – great fun for the children who took part.

The response to *Blue Peter*'s items about wild-life and the environment has proved beyond all doubt that children care passionately about these subjects. When it came to finding fresh ideas for *Animals Matter*, *Blue Peter* viewers did not let us down!

We had 41,657 pictures, poems, essays, re-ports, puzzles, games and recipes. We had ele-phants and emus, seals and Siamese, dormice and dodos and, of course, loads of puffins!

The judging was a nightmare! Major *Blue Peter* competitions are usually limited to pic-tures. With *Animals Matter*, we had to decide if a recipe was more worthy of a prize than a campaigning report, or if a poem was better than a picture. The judges – who included Yvette Fielding and John Leslie from *Blue Peter*, Liz Attenborough from Puffin and Tony Ross, who has provided many of the illustrations for the book – had enormous fun selecting the overall winners.

This book is the result. We hope you enjoy it.

Lewis Bronze,
Editor, *Blue Peter*,
July 1991

1

ANIMALS MATTER

Animals Matter

Animals matter,
They matter to me.
From the biggest whale.
To the tiniest flea.
Don't shoot them,
Pollute them,
Don't cut down their trees.
Animals matter,
Look after them PLEASE!

1ST PRIZEWINNER – 7s and under

AMY FERGUSON   AGE 7   OMAGH, CO. TYRONE, N. IRELAND

Five Facts on Endangered Animals

Did you know that 100 pandas starved to death in the 1970s?

Did you know that in the past 50 years the number of tigers in Asia has gone down from about 100,000 to about 5,000?

Did you know that the Asian elephants have been hunted for several thousand years, whereas the African species has only been hunted with any intensity for just over the last two centuries?

Did you know that gorillas are almost exclusively vegetarian in their diet?

Did you know that throughout the world, 50 acres of jungle is cleared every minute?

Well, now you DO know!

HELEN SYMS   AGE 9   WARRINGTON, CHESHIRE

Animal Extinction

If you don't listen now
your favourite animal might
become EXTINCT!
Whether it's a tiger, lion,
elephant or giant panda
cos you won't get a second
chance later. So LISTEN now.
In a blink of an eye another
elephant will die. With a
splash of a tail we will lose
another whale. In the black

night sky more tigers will die.
In the throw of a net we will lose
more dolphins yet.
If you don't act now
your favourite animal might
become EXTINCT!
Whether it's a tiger, lion,
elephant or giant panda
cos you won't get a second
chance later. So ACT now.

SARAH BURKE   AGE 6   MARLOW, BUCKS.

KAREN ENDEAN   AGE 11   BROCKENHURST, HANTS.

Animal Alphabet

A is for apes, big, strong and bold,
B is for bats, with poor sight, we are told,
C is for cuckoos, expressing their call,
D is for doves, bringing peace to us all,
E is for elephants, under a threat,
F is for fishes, avoiding the net,
G is for giraffes, proud heads everywhere,
H is for humming-birds, poised in mid-air,
I is for insects, so busy all day,
J is for jaguars, stalking their prey,
K is for kangaroos, hopping and bouncing,
L is for larks, distant songs they're
  announcing,
M is for monkeys, jumping and swinging,
N is for nightingales, so sweetly singing,
O is for owls, out through all the night weathers,
P is for peacocks, showing off their fine
  feathers,
Q is for quails, protecting their eggs,
R is for rabbits, hopping on two legs,
S is for snakes, hissing and darting,
T is for tortoises, slowly departing,
U is for unicorns, seen only in books,
V is for vultures, with peculiar looks,
W is for wolves, howling in packs,
X is for xenosaurus, with speckledy backs,
Y is for yak, with horns like two pipes,
Z is for zebra, with black and white stripes.
H is for HUMANS, hunting and killing,
  destroying the forests and rivers they're
  filling.

Now let's join together, avoiding bloodshed,
And save all the animals, A to Z.

MATTHEW SPINK   AGE 11   SCARBOROUGH, N. YORKS.

2ND RESERVE – 11s to 15s

ANDREW HARROLD   AGE 11   WOKING, SURREY

animals matter because
if all animals die out
then people will die out
too

*LINDA JOY BIRKIN   AGE 5   WOLLATON PARK,
NOTTINGHAM*

Make Your Own Animal Badge

WHAT YOU NEED
- ⋆ Piece of blank paper
- ⋆ Tracing paper
- ⋆ Coloured pencils or felt-tips
- ⋆ Piece of cardboard on which to mount the badge (a cereal packet is ideal)

* Scissors
* 1 safety-pin
* Glue
* Sticky tape

HOW TO MAKE YOUR BADGE
1. Using the tracing paper, draw round the badge on the previous page.
2. Shade in the design on the back of the tracing paper, then transfer the design on to the blank sheet.
3. Colour in the badge (use any colours you wish).
4. With scissors, cut round the finished design.
5. Glue the design on to a piece of cardboard.
6. Cut round the circular shape of the design.
7. Get an adult to help you and attach the safety-pin to the back of the cardboard using sticky tape, as illustrated below.

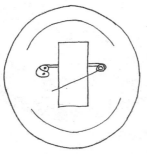

Now that you have completed your badge you can wear it with pride and help others become aware that ANIMALS MATTER.

PAUL JACKSON   AGE 13   MAGHULL, MERSEYSIDE

Conservation Box

CLUES

Across

1. The stoat-like animal killed for its thick brown fur (4)
4. To pursue and kill (4)
6. The peregrine _ _ _ _ _ _ is much used for hawking (6)
7. An animal which lives in a sett (6)
8. A friendly sea mammal considered a pest by tuna fishermen (7)
10. A black and white bird with a brightly-coloured bill (6)
11. The largest sea mammal (5)

14. 'Jaws' (5)
15. A large cat with a stripy coat (5)
16. As dead as a _ _ _ _ (4)
18. An elephant's tusk is made of (5)
19. Contamination caused by mankind (9)

Down

2. 'Royal' blue bird that eats freshwater fish (10)
3. Rain that destructs vegetation (4, 4)
5. Gull-like marine bird – to twist? (4)
7. A whale's fat (7)
9. As blind as a _ _ _ (3)
12. A species no longer existing (7)
13. An animal killed for its tusks (8)
17. A nocturnal bird which screeches and hoots (3)

Answers on page 154

Answers on page 154

FAITH EVANS   AGE 14   HAVERFORDWEST,
PEMBROKESHIRE

We Couldn't Live Without Them

This is a story about the day the animals went on strike.

The people laughed; one man said, 'It won't make any difference to us!'

Well that's what they thought!

Next morning . . . 'Why's my toast dry?'
'Why's my coffee black?'

'Mummy, I've got dry cereal.'

'Well dears, the cows are on strike, so there is no milk for cereal and coffee! And without milk there is no butter, we will just have to manage as best we can.'

Meanwhile, at the wool factory . . . 'None of us will get paid today.'

'Why?'

'The sheep are all on strike!'

In other parts of the town the police couldn't work because the horses and dogs were on strike. The blind people couldn't leave their houses and flats because the guide-dogs were on strike.

And they all realized they couldn't live without them.

KELLY RUTTER   AGE 8   DENTON, MANCHESTER

Letter From an Animal

Dear Editor,

I am writing in to voice my opinion on humans, for a change. We are supposed to be inferior, you are supposed to be in charge. Huh, some job you're doing!

Take fox-hunting for an example. That's really preserving the wildlife! Hey, and what about leaving us some space? I know you need somewhere to live as well, but it needn't mean bulldozing our homes down. Don't humans get notified or moved when demolition takes place?

Then there's the problem of pollution! Wouldn't you get just a little bit annoyed if someone chucked toxic waste in your bath? Of course you would, so why chuck it in the sea?!

I'd also like to make a point about your immoral taste in clothes! If God had intended you to wear fur for fun he'd have given it to you! So leave seals, foxes, mink, musquash, moles, ermine, squirrels, etc. alone! It's not just fur you seem to hanker after either. There's ivory, leather, suede, and I could go further!

I know that in a sense we were created with the use of food in mind, but is it too much to ask you to be not quite so greedy and kill what you need rather than unnecessarily wasting animal lives by shooting for fun. I'm sure you'd consider it great fun if we took up 'killing humans' as our hobby, 'just to fill up the odd five minutes'!

What I'd also like to know is what your reaction would be if you came home to discover your baby stolen. It would be horrific wouldn't it? Right, well remember that next time you're tempted to bring home one of those 'pretty speckled eggs', it used to be a life!

Something else I don't understand about humans is your vanity. You're so desperate to look good that you willingly sacrifice animals every day just to make sure that the one millionth and fifty-sixth new brand of lipstick is safe!

Look what a mess you've made of the world. Was it animals that made the hole in the ozone layer? Did *we* cause the greenhouse effect? No! But look, it isn't just you that is suffering as a result! What about us – inferior as we may be – we still exist!

I would, however, like to end on a more optimistic note. So would you mind leaving me a couple of minutes, no – make that days, to think of something good you've done!

Yours respectfully,

A very frustrated member of the so called 'inferior' animal race!

PS I don't know why I put respectfully. What have you done to give me cause to respect you?

ELIZABETH GREEN   AGE 14   STOCKPORT, CHESHIRE

If Only

If only they would all stop chopping down
    trees
Polluting our rivers and oceans and seas
If only they stopped hunting us for our skins
Crocodile bags, throw them all in the bins

If only they didn't buy ivory things
Elephants really would start prospering
If only our fur coats rich folk didn't need
Then we would be spared, it's only their greed
If only they didn't cast drift-nets to fish
Dolphins and whales would get their biggest
    wish
If only they didn't spoil hedgerows and land
Wouldn't the time for our wildlife be grand?
If only they were kind to all of their pets
We animals wouldn't have any more threats
If only the humans would all stop to think
Before they make all of us nearly extinct
'Cause animals matter an awful lot too
We were here on this earth long before you.

IAN MCPHEE   AGE 9   CROWBOROUGH, E. SUSSEX

MICHAEL JONES   AGE 13   SOLIHULL, W. MIDLANDS

Animal Puzzles

1. WORDSEARCH

B	A	D	G	E	R	F	O	X	N
R	T	I	B	B	A	R	L	E	B
O	G	T	E	S	A	E	W	Y	R
T	O	A	N	N	C	T	R	E	A
A	R	W	N	A	D	T	H	K	U
G	F	O	T	K	H	O	A	N	G
I	I	C	I	E	R	P	G	O	A
L	T	W	G	S	I	E	E	M	J
L	I	A	E	G	W	H	A	L	E
A	G	O	R	I	L	L	A	Z	E

Can you find all these animals in the
wordsearch above?

Alligator	Elephant	Kiwi	Rat
Badger	Fly	Lion	Snake
Bat	Fox	Monkey	Tiger
Bear	Frog	Newt	Whale
Cat	Gorilla	Otter	
Cow	Horse	Pig	
Dog	Jaguar	Rabbit	

Unused letters spell another animal.

2. ANIMAL RIDDLE

Each line of this riddle will lead you to a different letter of the alphabet. Put the letters together and you will find the answer.

My first is in SHEEP but not in FLEECE
My second is in BEAR but not in FUR
My third is in KANGAROO but not in
   POUCH
My fourth is in BIRD but not in BEAK
My fifth is in CAMEL but not in HUMP
My whole is black and white and becoming
   extinct

Answers on pages 154–5

HANNAH PEARCE   AGE 14   CULLOMPTON, DEVON

Animals Have Rights Too!

Animals have been here much longer than man,
But try to make sense of this (if you can):
They're treated like they shouldn't exist,
What kind of people would do this?
           – YOUR PEOPLE

Elephants are killed just for their ivory,
Selfish people use it to make things like jewellery
Before we know it all the elephants will be gone
What sort of world would let the suffering go on?
           – YOUR WORLD

Testing cosmetics on animals is really cold-
  hearted,
I can't understand why it was ever started,
Killing life for beauty is *very* unnecessary,
Which continents allow this brutality?
                    – YOUR CONTINENT

Circuses claim to be 'fun' for all ages,
But what about the animals crushed into
  cages?
'Fun' for you is pure loneliness and misery for
  them,
Where is this cruelty allowed to happen?
                    – YOUR COUNTRY

Imagine being killed just for your fur to be
  worn,
Rich ladies queue up to buy them to 'keep
  them warm',
Millions of animals are killed for this each
  year,
Where does it happen (if it's not already clear)?
                    – YOUR CITY

Having read this poem, please listen to me,
Have a heart and choose cruelty-free.
But who's the one who can make the decision
Between their extinction or their preservation?
                    – YOU

REBECCA DAVIDSON   AGE 14   OVERIJSE, BELGUIM

2

SAVE OUR SEA-LIFE

Whales – here today GONE tomorrow!

Whales are getting killed every minute, they are killed for their meat and blubber (fat), they are killed with harpoons. I don't see why they should be killed because they are lovely creatures. Let me tell you about them. Whales live in lots of seas. They eat plankton, they are quite harmless really, even though they are very big. The biggest whale ever is a Blue Whale which can grow to over 30 metres long and can weigh over 100 tonnes. The body of a whale is streamlined (smooth and curved) so that they can move easily through the water. It swims by beating its tail up and down. Whales have no fur and are kept warm by a thick layer of fat (blubber) under the skin. A whale's nostrils are on the top of its head. As the whale breathes out or blows, a puff of vapour appears. This is rather like the way your breath steams on a cold day.

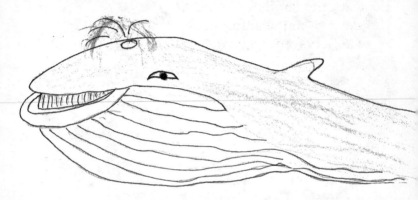

JENNIFER BULLOCK   AGE 9   NETTLEHAM, LINCOLN

The Whale

Far below the breaking waves,
Deep within the heart of the ocean, swims a
   gentle giant,
One of the last
Of a dying race.
With mighty beauty unparalleled he travels,
Cruising with the currents, drifts and flows,
Then breaking to the golden surface,
Stealing the arena of air as he pierces the
   water,

A great fount soars like a geyser,
And he has been seen.
The harpoon closes as his tail hits the water,
Breaks through skin as he desperately tries to
    dive,
But his fate is decided,
To them he is just a commodity,
Just so much more money,
Food for the family.
His race will not last forever.
How long before the waters no longer crash
At the power of his kind?
They will not last forever,
Not in our world.
Not unless we change.

PAUL MCDERMOTT   AGE 13   EARL SHILTON, LEICESTER

'What Am I?'

I am shy, that is why I hide.
Although I can grow over 20 feet I am not a
    MONSTER!
I eat crab . . . YUM YUM!
I change shape and colour.
I have tentacles that help me climb.
There are 150 different species of us.
I have blue blood.
We are related to snails.

Answer on page 155

JESSICA COLLINS   AGE 9   CAWSANDS, CORNWALL

Friendly giants of the deep
Whales may cry while we sleep
Suffering pain from spears that fly
I don't think they need to die!

LENA TURTON   AGE 14   BURTON-ON-TRENT, STAFFS.

Saving Seals

I am a seal, all alone
As my mother has been taken
By the Humans.
I am washed up on the beach
And a Human is coming with a barking dog,
It frightens me and I cry.
I try to get back in the water,
But I hurt my flipper on a hidden rock.
There is no escape from the beach,
The dog, or the Human.
Suddenly, strong hands lift me and carry me
    away.
I shut my eyes, scared and lonely.
When I open my eyes, I am in a pool
With another seal.
She comes to me and welcomes me,
Then tells me I'm in a seal sanctuary.
'Don't worry, the Humans here won't hurt
    you.
They look after you and feed you,
And let you go when you're better.'
Later, a Human comes in and gently lifts me
And takes me to another pool.
I see more seals, happily playing
And dive into the water.
Then I see my mother, and tears come to my
    eyes.
I swim to her and she sees me.
We joyfully embrace and tell each other our
    stories.
Weeks later, together again, we are finally freed

And swim in the beautiful ocean
That is our home.

SUSANNA LUTMAN   AGE 10   BEESTON, NOTTS.

Message in a Bottle

Dear Humans

Hello, I'm a dolphin and I'm going to tell you
about the time when my friends got captured
in some awful nets which were lowered to the
bottom of the sea. It happened when we were
going to find some fish. When we saw lots of
good fish we raced over before they could get
away but we did not see the net and got caught.
The sailors who were holding the net pulled it
up with my friends, so that's why I'm sending
this message. You are the humans and you can
get rid of the nets so please save us dolphins.

From Daniella the Dolphin.

CLAIRE HOLLYWELL   AGE 7   HORSHAM, W. SUSSEX

The Day I Lost Mum

Mum screeches to tell me to move closer to
her side. I obey, as I have done since we
started the migration south – since leaving the
warm waters of the Indian Ocean several
months ago, not long after my birth.

Mum spurs me on to keep up with the rest
of the school. The days are long now and food

(plankton) which colours the ice-floes yellow is in abundance in these cold Antarctic waters.

Beware! of killer whales, Mum says, who would just like to catch a humpback pup such as myself alone. They feed higher up the food-chain and I would definitely be on their menu along with pups of our cousins the blue and bluefin. But the creature which poses the greatest threat to us and our environment rides above the waves.

A long dark shadow cast over us as we ascended to exhale and take a deep breath of clean Antarctic air. A loud 'BANG' rang out and, shortly after, I lost Mum forever!

LUCYANN SUTTON   AGE 10   MIDDLESBROUGH,
CLEVELAND

The Dolphins' Tale

Dolphins are playing, jumping and leaping in
  the deep blue sea.
The fishermen come and catch them in their
  big drift-net!
Please! Please! Let them swim free!
Stop Mr Fisherman! We just want to be
  friends, can't you see?
Tomorrow there will be nothing left in our seas.
Stop! Stop! Mr Fisherman.
Leave us be
To swim free in the deep blue sea.

JESSICA ROWLEY   AGE 6   CAMBERLEY, SURREY

3

ELEPHANTS, RHINOS AND BIG CATS

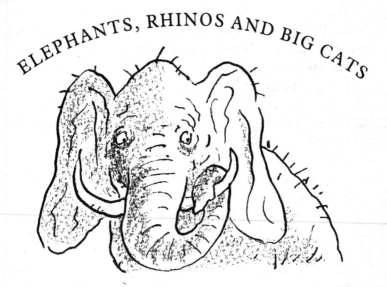

ENDANGERED SPECIES~

The elephant

Zoe 1992.

THERE ARE TWO MAIN TYPES OF ELEPHANTS:

African   Indian

THE AFRICAN CAN GROW UP TO 4 METRES HIGH AND CAN WEIGH UP TO 6 TONNES.

1 PRIZE

IT IS NOT TO BE CONFUSED WITH THE SPECIES:- charlesphant.

THE PURPOSE OF THE ELEPHANTS BIG EARS IS TO KEEP THEM COOL.

(although some prefer to use modern technology).

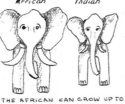

WRINKLE CREAM IS NOT AVAILABLE WHERE THE ELEPHANTS LIVE, SO INSTEAD THEY SPEND HOT AFTERNOONS WALLOWING IN MUD.

ELEPHANTS SLEEP STANDING UP BECAUSE A BED ISN'T BIG ENOUGH FOR THEM.

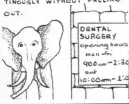

1ST PRIZEWINNER – 11s to 15s

ZOË SMITH   AGE 14   CLIFTONWOOD, BRISTOL

The Elephant – 'The Endangered Species'

One of the most serious problems for the elephant is poaching. At the moment some 50,000 animals a year are killed because of poaching. If poaching doesn't stop within 20 years the African Elephant, unfortunately, could become extinct.

In 1989 the world finally woke up to what was happening to Africa's elephants. Their numbers had plummeted from an estimated 1.3 million to 609,000 in just ten years. The main cause was poaching for ivory. Up to 100,000 elephants were being slaughtered every year, their front teeth hacked out, their bodies left to rot, their tiny calves left to die of starvation. The unthinkable was suddenly being talked about – extinction.

Ivory is not a rock or a wood, it is a dead elephant's tooth. And as long as there is a demand for the ivory ear-rings, bangles, statuettes and knick-knacks that adorn the wealthy and their homes, someone is going to go out and kill elephants to get a share of that wealth.

Already attitudes are changing. In May 1989 Tanzania was the first nation to propose a ban on the ivory trade, and the ELEFRIENDS campaign was launched in London. In July of the same year Kenyan President Daniel Arap Moi bravely burned 12 tonnes of confiscated ivory, proving to the world that he was serious about ending the ivory trade, and in October the nations on CITES voted for a ban on ivory.

The ivory trade grew steadily between 1950 when 204 tonnes of tusks were sold and 1983 when the figure was 1,000 tonnes. The annual total then began to fall: 600 tonnes in 1986; 300 tonnes in 1987. But this did not mean that fewer elephants were being killed. In 1979 one tonne of ivory represented 54 dead elephants – mainly bulls. By 1987 most mature bulls had been shot, and so cows and calves were being killed for their smaller tusks. One tonne of ivory in 1987 came from 113 dead elephants, and many of them were adult females, so a further 55 calves, with no ivory, were left to die of starvation. If something is not done to stop the ivory trade, the trade will end itself before too long by wiping out the source of its raw material.

Something must be done now before the elephant, a beautiful and loving creature, will be wiped off the face of the earth, never to be seen again. There is no question about it, the ivory trade must be stopped, now, before it is too late.

EMILY KEIGHLEY   AGE 14   LONGRIDGE, LANCS.

Elephants

Elephants are gigantic. Baby elephants are small but they are bigger than me. An elephant's skin is all screwed up like prunes or paper made into a ball. Their trunks are long. Grown up elephants have sharp tusks. They feel like smooth stones or like plastic. They have big round feet and big toe-nails too but

they can't run fast because they are too heavy.
They have long, thin tails with fluff on the
end and baby elephants hold on to them with
their trunks like I hold my mummy's hand.

SARAH COTGREAVE   AGE 5   ST IVES, CAMBS.

Elephants

Elephants are nice, but they
Live in danger,
Even though they don't do any harm.
People must be thoughtful and make the
Hunters stop,
And ivory should not be bought.
Now is the time to care about elephants
Then when we grow up our children will
See them.

CAROLINE DAVISON   AGE 6   PURLEY, SURREY

The Elephant

Look at the elephant big and grey.
He lives in Africa, far away.
His skin is wrinkled, his trunk is too;
I know it is, I've seen one in the zoo.
The elephant's tusks are long and curved.
They take years to grow so I've heard.
Look at the hunter small and sly,
Shoots the elephant – do you know why?
To steal the tusks to sell to others
Who make the trinkets that are sold
    undercover.
Look at the elephant on the ground,
All his family gathered around; see the sadness
    in their eyes.
Now the hunter has gone away,
Lives to hunt another day.
Stop this killing, stop the madness,
Put an end to all the sadness.

ALISON MERRETT   AGE 8   PONTARDULAIS,
W. GLAMORGAN

The Worst Day Ever

Maybe we wouldn't have been so enthusiastic
if we'd known what had been waiting for us.
Everything began like normal when we arrived
at our favourite feeding ground after walking
across Africa for months and months.

   We arrived early that morning all cheerful at
the thought of eating the fresh luscious
vegetation. There were eight of us, and we split

into two groups of four. I went with my mother, father and aunt to the water-hole full of enthusiasm, for we had had no drink for three days. While we were bathing in the turquoise water and splashing around happily, we did not hear the booming of gun-fire as our fellow elephants were being shot for their ivory tusks in the feeding ground.

We left the water-hole full of delicious water and joy, but as we neared the feeding ground we could all sense that something was wrong, there was no noise of the bark being pulled off the trees as elephants normally would do when they return to their feeding grounds.

We entered the feeding place cautiously wondering what to expect. Then we stopped dead, our fellow elephants were all lying on the floor with blood gushing from bullet holes and where their tusks had once been.

My mother pushed me away from the horrific scene and beckoned me to go back to the water-hole with her. My father and aunt stayed with the corpses and did the ritual that all elephants instinctively do.

My mother and I were half-way to the water-hole when we heard two shots. Immediately we both rushed back, but I was too young and small to keep up with my mother. I caught up with her just in time to see her being shot, right in the heart. She fell to the floor beside my dead aunt. I began to move towards her but I heard rustling in the undergrowth and some poachers crept out. I edged back just far enough for me to see them pulling tusks out. These brutal murderers were slashing away at my fellow elephants' rough skins to get their tusks out.

Two minutes later they had driven off with seven pairs of tusks and I was left with seven corpses of my dead family. I began the ritual on my mother, and as I did so I saw a tear come to her eye and trickle down her face, to the ground.

KERRY WATTS   AGE 15   READING, BERKS.

A Day in the Life of a Rhino

After a good night's sleep I woke and looked around me; the sun was gradually rising, getting hotter every hour. I decided on a simple breakfast of grass and water from a nearby river which was slowly but surely drying up, as summer had approached.

Munching the grass, and debating whether to go and see Uncle Cuthbert, I gazed around me and looked at my home. My neighbours were declining, the numbers of us Sumatran rhinos disappearing. I think there was only around 750 of us left. Each day one or two more vanished. Yesterday, my best friend, Harry, went. I found his body, with a sawn off tusk, in a heap, vultures circling above me ready to eat Harry. I was so angry!!

There are some nice people, though, wanting to protect us. They are called the SRT (Save

Rhino Trust). They do a good job and take us to National Parks, where we can enjoy freedom, but we are more protected.

This afternoon, having come back from seeing Uncle Cuthbert, I decided on a nice doze in the shade and found a cool place near some bushes, rather withered and burnt, but cool. I dreamt.

Suddenly I heard humans running through the grasses. I heard a cry from a rhino; I knew then the poachers had come! Run! I thought, but my feet felt rigid and stuck to the ground; run, go on, run. I had to, for my life. I heard the piercing noise of the electric saw in my ears; another cry. I ran then, for my life, faster and faster. But where could I run to?

I felt something sharp and painful hit my side and without warning I fell to the ground. The next thing I knew, I was awake and being enticed into a big truck. I saw Uncle Cuthbert and decided this was animal heaven. But after seeing the humans I realized I'd been drugged and taken to a big truck, and then been given an antidote, and was on my way to a National Park like I'd been told. I was so glad I wasn't going to contribute to the £250,000,000 made by poachers for ivory.

NAOMI DAGLEY   AGE 13   AUDENSHAW, MANCHESTER

MONSTERS ARE A FIGMENT OF YOUR IMAGINATION

SOON THIS RHINO WILL BE TOO!

ROBIN PAVIER   AGE 10   CLIFTON GROVE, NOTTINGHAM

Animals Matter

Ten black rhinos were happy in the sun
Along came poachers and then there were
none.

Nine playful dolphins cruising free
Thirty-mile-long fishing-nets left none to see.

Eight clever cormorants fishing in the waves
One stinking oil-slick puts them in their
graves.

Seven lofty rain forests the home of countless
creatures
Hacked and burned because of greed are now
just bygone features.

Six gentle spouting sperm whales saw no need
to flee
But breathed their last with the harpoon blast
in the blood-red boiling sea.

Five clumsy natterjacks tried to cross the road
One big juggernaut left no trace of toad.

Four lively otters in the river were well fed
Herbicides and pesticides soon had them dead.

Three wise old barn-owls used to swoop at
night
Destruction of their habitat put them out of
flight.

Two tusks of ivory on an elephant belong
Not in the hands of carvers in downtown Hong
Kong.

One polluted lifeless world spinning round in
   space
Is this to be the legacy for the human race?

EVA ASKHAM-SPENCER   AGE 11   FAREHAM, HANTS.

Cheetah in the Safari Park

We went to the safari park, my family and I,
The first thing we saw was a bird that couldn't
   fly.
The next was a lion – a mountainous beast,
If we'd got out of the car we'd have been his
   feast.

We then saw a cheetah as swift as a bird,
He was going so fast his image was blurred.
Then suddenly he raced up to the car,
His nimble feet pounding against the hard tar.

Those gigantic jaws he opened up wide,
I was so scared I wanted to hide.
What had happened, had we made him mad?
But then I saw his eyes and they looked . . .
   well . . . sad.

The cheetah I saw was trapped without bars,
He was kept in the park like insects in jars.
In that sea of cars he searches in vain,
Searching for someone to ease his pain.

ALEXANDER BOTTOMORE   AGE 11   MANSFIELD, NOTTS.

An Open Letter

To those that care,

I would have thought that being the fastest land animal in the world would secure my species' future, but we are now so few that, on average, there is only one cheetah per 600 square miles of African land. The problem is not that we can't catch our prey, but that there isn't any prey to catch. When we do make a kill, it is often stolen by other 'big cats' such as lions and leopards.

That isn't our only problem though, as our fur coat is very valuable, and although we can run very fast, we cannot outrun a bullet. But it is not only the adults that are in danger, so are our cubs. To catch a cub, as they are caught, not killed, a poacher follows a travelling family until one or more cubs tire and drop behind the rest, and then picks them up. Over 100 cubs a year are taken in this way, and every one of them is valuable to our continuing existence.

The only place that we survive in significant figures is the Kundelungu National Park. The main reason is that there is a lot of prey. So it seems that we are dying out because our prey is dying out. Well, I don't know whether you can help us or not, but if you can, we really need it.

Yours, with hope, The Cheetahs

TAMSIN SCOTT   AGE 13   EAST MALLING, KENT

SARA TOWNSEND-CARTWRIGHT AGE 12 EARLSDON,
COVENTRY

The Lion

I woke up and gave a big roar,
I walked round the cage and this is what I saw:
Cameras clicking all the time,
Oh, how I wish it was breakfast time.
Suddenly the keeper comes with a piece of meat,
Then everyone comes to watch me eat.

I lie down and start to dream,
I wish I was in the wild next to a stream.
From the people getting no bother,
I would roam freely around the wilderness,
Even play-fighting with the lioness.

I prowl around the cage, it is nearly dinner-
    time,
I see a bird on my cage and think, that is
    mine.
I have the same food every day,
I think I should have my own say,
I hope one day I will get my teeth around a
    nice juicy deer,
But I still enjoy my meat here.

Where I am I lie and stare,
At the penguins splashing in their own lair.
When I am bored I climb up the tree,
It reminds me of where I should be,
It puts me in a good mood,
And always makes me ready for food.

The sun goes behind a cloud,
The zoo is quiet, no longer loud,
I go to my bed to get some sleep,
At the penguins I have another peep,
I am lonely but warm in my cage.
I don't really mind, I can survive,
Because I am here for the rest of my life.

LOUISE WARD   AGE 13   THETFORD, NORFOLK

4

MONKEYS AND PANDAS

Sally the Monkey

I am a cheeky monkey
Climbing up a tree.
You humans are not fast enough
To catch poor little me.

My babby's name is Sally,
I think she's very cute.
I bet you'd love to catch her
And put her in a suit.

You'd put her in a nappy
And sit her on your lap,
And feed her far too much,
Until she got too fat.

Or would you put her in a zoo
And make her sad and fret?
Please leave her with her mommy
Or she will get upset.

3RD PRIZEWINNER – 8s, 9s and 10s

LISA WILSON   AGE 10   MINWORTH, SUTTON COLDFIELD

Save Me

I am a little baby chimp,
but now I have a name.
I was kidnapped from my homeland,
and now humans have made me tame.
To capture me they killed my mum,
they did it with a gun.
I fell to the ground to be put in a box,
for days I saw no sun.
Illegally exported, I very nearly died.
Now I'm sold to a man who takes pictures
I cannot be camera-shy.
Tourists pay to pose with me,
but I cannot put up a fight.
You see, when they sold me,
I was left with no teeth that could bite.
Others of my kind end up in laboratories,
tested with humans' disease.
We had no choice, but humans
won't you listen to our pleas!
Leave us alone, please let us be.
We belong in our jungle not on TV!

KELLY BINGHAM   AGE 11   PLYMOUTH, DEVON

Monkeys – We Need Them!

O	R	A	N	G	O	U	T	A	N	G
Z	E	Y	P	Q	Y	U	H	R	R	A
X	V	E	M	A	N	D	R	I	L	L
M	M	D	Z	F	L	G	A	B	C	L
F	A	G	V	N	M	A	L	D	L	I
R	G	R	D	B	A	B	O	O	N	R
L	E	C	M	D	U	P	H	O	M	O
H	A	D	K	O	Y	V	M	R	C	G
F	M	V	I	B	S	W	X	I	L	V
G	L	B	D	P	X	E	N	O	H	F
R	H	E	S	U	S	Z	T	R	L	C

Can you find 8 kinds of monkey?

Gorilla
Orang-outang
Baboon
Spider
Chimpanzee
Mandrill
Rhesus
Marmoset

Answers on page 155

JOHN ROWLEY   AGE 6   WORCESTER

Don't Let the Pandas Die

Pandas are not very colourful.
They are only black and white.
But there isn't enough food
For every panda in the world.

Pandas live in China.
The weather suits them there.
But there isn't enough food
For every panda in the world.

Pandas like bamboo shoots.
They gobble them up every day.
But there isn't enough food
For every panda in the world.

Pandas are rather special.
I think they should survive.
How can we find enough food
For every panda in the world?

3RD PRIZEWINNER – 7s and under

ELEANOR BAGG   AGE 6   WEYMOUTH, DORSET

Panda News

Pandas are large, black and white, bear-like animals. Pandas carry their babies on their backs while climbing, walking, etc. They eat bamboo leaves or bamboo shoots. They are originally found in the Himalayas of Tibet but they are also found in China and Russia. But most pandas are found in zoos around the world.

People have many different methods of trapping pandas, such as a hidden cage with bamboo leaves or bamboo shoots inside it, and when a panda comes to eat them the cage door is closed and locked. Then the cage is carried to a truck and then often flown to a foreign zoo. But sometimes traps go wrong and a panda's life is lost. Pandas are not usually treated well on the journey, and by the time the journey is over many of the pandas are dead!

This is called captivity, a dreaded word for animal lovers and animals. It's now illegal to trap pandas but it's still going on. Pandas are an endangered species of animal and are protected, but somehow their numbers are still going down. Most of the pandas still alive are in zoos.

People are also cutting down bamboo trees for farmland and building-land and the wood is used for fuel or furniture and also sold to other countries. This destroys their shelter for the night and food. And if we don't act quickly there won't be any left in the wild.

And we'll have the blame for it! So don't wait any longer.

SKEVY GROUTARI   AGE 10   HATTON, DERBYS.

ANDREW ROBERTSON   AGE 7   CARRBRIDGE,
INVERNESS-SHIRE

Saving the Panda

For some time now, scientists have been worried about the number of pandas left. Every effort is being made to save the giant panda. Twelve panda reserves have been set up to give the last pandas a chance to live. Scientists are making careful studies of pandas' way of life. This will help them plan the best way to help them survive.

So stop and think – this animal really does matter.

NATALIE BROOME   AGE 10   WALSALL, W. MIDLANDS

The Panda – Gone Forever?

Animals are in a lot of trouble, and
If we don't start helping them now,
Soon will be gone forever and ever,
And not all man's technology can replace
    them.

I have only seen a panda on the TV,
And soon these will be gone too.
So my little sister will not even know
What a panda is. Whose fault will it be?

2ND PRIZEWINNER – 8s, 9s and 10s

SAM JOHNSON   AGE 8   SALTASH, CORNWALL

5

WILDLIFE NEARER HOME

Tadpoles

This is a true story
called Operation Save the Tadpoles.
There was a small pool in
the field by our house
with some tadpoles in it.
Mummy said it would
dry up and the tadpoles
would die. So we fished
them out just in time
as there was only a tiny
puddle left.

2ND PRIZEWINNER – 7s and under

PHILIPPA WILCOX   AGE 5   PONTYPOOL, GWENT

The Frog

The frog's worst enemy is close at hand,
With each new house we take their land.
Not only that, but without a quiver
We dump our sewage into their river.

A frog starts life as spawn near the surface,
Little will survive complete metamorphosis.
Despite the losses incurred at this stage,
The numbers ensure a few come of age.

Survival for tadpoles is hard every day,
The fish find them tasty and nice easy prey.
Not only fish, but birds as well,
Combine to make a tadpole's life hell.

The children come, with jars and nets,
Catch and entrap them and treat them like
    pets.
At first admired, and then forgotten,
Condemned to death they sink to the bottom.

The adult stage gives little protection,
The frogs are caught and used in dissection.
'Hands on' experience is good they say,
In spite of textbooks with picture display.

We must act now, so much is at stake,
How much more can our environment take?
No creature is safe, the large and the small,
And Man's selfish interest will cause their
    downfall.

CAROLINE HAYWOOD   AGE 13   WEST BRIDGFORD,
NOTTINGHAM

NATHAN BROADHEAD   AGE 11   ROTHERHAM, S. YORKS.

London's Wildlife

I live in London but . . .
Yesterday I saw a badger
I also saw some wild geese
My sister saw rabbits playing in the park

I live in London but . . .
Today Mummy saw a fox
And Daddy showed me frog-spawn
The dog chased a squirrel up a tree

I live in London but . . .
Tomorrow I hope to see stoats
Or even otters by the river
I live in London and so does wildlife

I wrote this because
last year I moved to
London. I didn't want
to but . . .
Wildlife can be everywhere if you
look after it!

BEN FRANCIS   AGE 6   RADLETT, HERTS.

Badgers

I like badgers
They come out at night
They look for food to eat
There are not many left because
naughty people kill them
I wish there were more
I like their stripy faces

EMMA KIRBY   AGE 6   GOOLE, N. HUMBERSIDE

Otters

There are two types of otters – the Asian otter
and the European otter. The European otter is
under threat. In Britain and elsewhere its
habitat is being destroyed owing to the

pollution of rivers. Such pollution affects their food supply by killing suitable prey. Also the trees along the rivers can die. The roots of these trees in the banks provide sheltered

homes and nesting places for the otters. Otters are now being bred in sanctuaries and reserves and then released back into the wild in suitable areas. They are very active creatures and in captivity are fed four times a day on a mixture of whiting, mince, liver and heart.

The picture opposite shows the general shape of an otter. Its body is long and agile. Its legs are short and strong. The long, tapering tail is used for steering and the four webbed feet aid powerful and swift swimming.

LORNA WORKMAN   AGE 8   CARLUKE, LANARKSHIRE

The Tarka Trail

The Tarka Trail is situated in Devon and is a walk six miles long. It starts at the museum of outdoor life in Okehampton and finishes at the Finch Foundry Museum in Sticklepath. It has been made to protect otters, badgers, wagtails, dippers and also the kingfisher. The trail has been named after the book called *Tarka the Otter*. In chapter 11, Tarka the otter had a fierce fight with Swaydagger and his bloodthirsty fellow stoats. There is also the Tarka Line which is a railway line that runs from Exeter to Barnstaple. The animals do not mind the noise of the train, as they have grown accustomed to it. It is because of places like the Tarka Trail and the Tarka Line that otters are being saved and allowed to breed and live happily.

TIMOTHY WEBSTER   AGE 10   JACOBSTOW, CORNWALL

Paws and Claws

Can you tell which paw print was made by which animal?

SQUIRREL

MOUSE

FOX

CAT

DEER

BADGER

RABBIT

COW

HORSE

OTTER

OYSTER-CATCHER

Answer on page 155

WANDA BEASLEY   AGE 12   AYLESTONE, LEICESTER

Moles

My eyes are closed
My nose is good,
I don't mean to
Spoil your lawn,
I'm just looking
For food.

CHRISTOPHER GREENALL   AGE 10   BARTON-ON-SEA,
HANTS.

The Fox Cubs

Their mother had only gone for a few minutes,
but when she came back they were not there.

A couple of nature lovers were wandering in
the beautiful Surrey woodlands, when they
discovered the fox cubs. 'The poor things,
they've been abandoned. We must take them
home and look after them.'

Two of the offspring were awake and
fighting with each other, but the female cub
was asleep, so the animal lovers roused her
and cradled the three until they reached their
home.

The baby foxes were cared for with vigilance
and nearly every minute of every day a tender
eye was cast over them watchfully. The cubs
were fine, but a few days later the males started
getting destructive and the next day the female
joined in too.

The foxes were becoming more and more

boisterous every day and the nature lovers were at their wits' end. The animals had now torn their way out of their box in the kitchen and were making a meal out of tearing the wallpaper down and scarring the table and chairs. The animal lovers were heroes (or so they thought) and they had saved the mammals' lives; but had they?

As the foxes were strongly progressing, the do-gooders thought they had done their bit and that the young animals were strong enough to survive. So they discarded the three small mites close to where they had found them.

A few days later a family of four found a young fox. It was pitifully thin with grazes on its legs and face. However, as one of the children gently went to pick it up, it took a snap at her and tried to reach the safety of the undergrowth. The family instantly knew what to do. They cut their walk short and turned immediately home to phone the RSPCA.

The mother stated clearly where they had found the dying fox and the RSPCA went straight to the woodlands just outside Dorking, to investigate.

In a short while the RSPCA were on the site and easily found the fox . . . and her two brothers, each skin and bones with bad cuts and grazes.

The foxes were shortly put in pens next to each other, they were fed on the correct food, but not being hand reared and not really having any contact with the human world.

(You may think this was cruel but it was only teaching them to be scared of us and not think that every human was a friend.)

These foxes were lucky. In the end they were taken care of by the right people. After seven weeks of being looked after carefully, they were able to feed themselves and fend for themselves generally.

So who cared most, the nature lovers or the family?

STEFANIE HULBERT   AGE 12   DORKING, SURREY

A Fox's Tale

Tonight I was looking for prey outside my normal boundary as the voles, rabbits and things that I ate in my normal ground tasted plain. They probably wouldn't taste any different anywhere else, but it would be nice to have a longer walk than usual, although not so long that my vixen would come out searching for me. I was taking my stroll with my stomach full and minding my own business when pain burst down my right foreleg. It sent my body to the ground. I barked a helpless howl then closed my eyes, still breathing heavily. I heard a dog bark and the crunching of bracken and sticks. I was scared it would be the hunt, so I half opened my eyes. Then all the weight lifted from my leg and I was being carried to a small house. Inside were badgers with white bandages wrapped around their legs, other foxes, otters and all sorts of animals from large to small. He lifted me on to a table. He cleaned the cuts and bandaged my leg. He put me in a very comfortable bed. Straight away I went to sleep. In the morning I was fed well and so were the other animals. Then I was taken outside and my leg was exercised, went back in to sleep and so forth. This cycle carried on for a week or so. Then the day came for me to go. He put me down in the woods where he had found me. I tested my leg. As I set off to tell my beloved vixen what had happened, I thought 'To humans like him, animals DO matter.'

CARLY HALFORD   AGE 9   BRACKNELL, BERKS.

The Stag

The snow began to fall quickly, but silently,
The muddy prints of both animal and human
    soon to vanish,
I pulled my coat around me . . . tighter,
The wind cutting my cheeks, pulling my hair.

Was this a good idea to go walking in such
    weather?
I needed to escape the confines of my home,
    to be free in cold, fresh air.
All was silent, not even the flutter of a bird,
The trees were still, they had succumbed to
    the wilderness of white.

I walked on further.
Suddenly, a movement.

There, standing in majestic solitude, head held
    high, crowned by its antlers,
Stood the King of the Forest.
He had obviously strayed to the edge of the
    woods,
In search of food.
His powerful body, calm and still.
His eyes, trusting, but watchful.

The sun soon to rest, sank lower in the sky.
Silhouetting the proudest of beasts, content
    with his freedom.

JESSICA LAWTHER   AGE 14   HERTFORD, HERTS.

I wrote this poem because I feel it would be a
great shame if this magnificent animal should
become extinct by the increase in popularity of
stag hunting.

The Escargot Largo

I'm tired of hearing people say,
'You've got to save the whale.'
When no one seems to care about
My own species: the snail.

'What nasty things do people do
To snails?' I hear you utter.
But I'm sure you wouldn't like
To end up cooked in garlic butter.

We're trodden on, we're squished and
 squashed,
By children we're dissected,
So a mollusc revolution
Would not come unexpected.

Just leave us in your garden,
All alone amongst the weeds,
And humans please remember,
Even gastropods have needs.

KERRY ROBERRY   AGE 11   ASPLEY, NOTTINGHAM

Snail Spiral

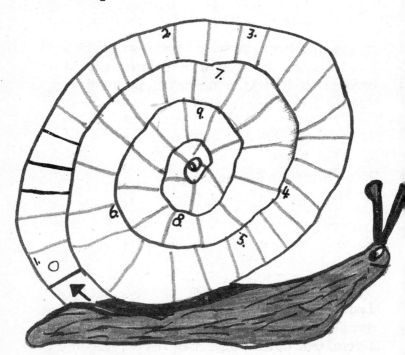

1. Ape with orange hair
2. Stinging insect
3. Freshwater reptile with a shell on its back
4. Small garden pond creature
5. Fruit-eating bird of the rain forest with a large coloured beak
6. Fish with a long bony horn
7. British bird with a head crest
8. A small dainty antelope
9. A very large mammal

Answers on page 155

WILLIAM FEEHALLY   AGE 9   HOUGHTON-ON-THE-HILL,
LEICS.

Worms

Worms are in the garden,
See them after the rain.
Don't stamp on them,
Don't slice them with your spade.
Don't be cruel
Or pick them up and kill them.
Be kind to worms.

REBECCA LAWTON   AGE 5   PONTEFRACT, W. YORKS.

Speaking of Worms

Long ago there was a garden that belonged to a gentle gardener. In the garden there lived a worm. One day the gardener was digging in the

mud to plant some sunflower seeds and then he
saw the worm. He put it back in the mud and
went inside for lunch. A blackbird came and
wanted the little worm for lunch, but the little
worm told him not to eat him because he helped
keep the garden clean and he was good for the
mud and he nibbled the leaves and let the water
drain through; and so the blackbird didn't eat
the little worm. And the little worm told the
blackbird not to eat him because the gardener
would feed him in the winter with some of his
brothers and sisters. Then the worm and the
blackbird became friends.

JOANNA DUCKWORTH AGE 6 WESTCLIFF-ON-SEA, ESSEX

My Grandad's Hedgehog

My grandad lives in a village in North
Yorkshire. When I went to stay with him he
told me about his friend a hedgehog who he
saw in his garden every night. One night we
were in bed and my grandad's hedgehog went
into my grandad's porch and went into a bag
with my daddy's shears in. When we woke up
it was the day that we were leaving. Daddy
packed the car and we were off, but nobody
knew the hedgehog was in the boot of the car.
We were back in London; still nobody had
found the hedgehog. It was sunny and we had

the door open and the windows open. Nobody
was looking and it went behind the curtains,
and still nobody found it. Mummy and Daddy
went to bed and then something super
happened. It went upstairs and went into my
mummy and daddy's room and woke them up.
My daddy took it carefully downstairs and put
it outside.

NICHOLAS PENNY   AGE 6   RUISLIP, MIDDLESEX

JENNY BALEMAN   AGE 13   LODDON, NORWICH

The Trials of Life (As Seen by a Hedgehog)

BEN BROCKBANK   AGE 14   HUDDERSFIELD, W. YORKS.

The Hedgehog

The hedgehog is an insect-eating mammal. There are over 15 species of hedgehog. The hedgehog is 25 to 30 centimetres long. It has a tail which is 2.5 to 3 centimetres long and can hardly be seen.

The hedgehog weighs 800 to 1200 grammes. His spines stick out in all directions, so it is impossible to handle a hedgehog that has rolled itself into a ball without being pricked.

The hedgehog is in danger from foxes and badgers as well as some birds of prey. But its most terrible enemy is the motor car. Every year, thousands of hedgehogs are killed on the roads. The hedgehog lives for eight to ten years.

CHRISTOPHER DAWSON   AGE 12   RATTLESDEN, SUFFOLK

JESSICA CARSEN   AGE 12   BURY ST. EDMUNDS, SUFFOLK

Stop! Danger!

Spiky, round and prickly
The hedgehog sniffs along,
Scurrying, snuffling, scuttling,
Looking for some food.
Stop! Danger! A predator is coming!
Roll up into a ball, little hedgehog.
Soft and comfy inside,
Jaggy and sharp outside,
Like spears to frighten the fox away.
Slowly the hedgehog comes out of his ball.
Back legs out. Front legs out.
Head pops out. All clear. Good!
Off he goes again,
Scurrying, snuffling, scuttling,
Looking for some food.

DANIEL FAIRBAIRN   AGE 6   AUCHTERMUCHTY, FIFE

About St. Tiggywinkle's Hospital

One day when my daddy went to London he
bought me a hedgehog puppet. Inside the
hedgehog's box was a leaflet that tells you
about Henry H. Hogg's club. I wanted to find
out more about the club so I wrote in and
joined the club. Then later in the year they
sent me a leaflet saying I could be in the
Tiggy's Club (that helps to save wildlife) if I
paid £6 or more. I joined that club as well.
Then I started to collect money at school. In
the end I collected £2.68. I sent it to the

Tiggy's Club and they sent me lots of information about hedgehogs and other patients they have got at the hospital, like Curly the fox. When I sent away the money I made a collecting money-box. The thing that made me join is that I love wildlife and my favourite animal is the hedgehog and the money goes to a good cause. If you want to join the Tiggy's Club the address is: Tiggy's Club, St. Tiggywinkle's Wildlife Hospital, 1 Pemberton Close, Aylesbury, Bucks HP21 7NY.

KATY PEVERILL   AGE 8   HANWORTH, NORFOLK

VICKY SOUTHERN   AGE 4   PRESTON, LANCS.

Insects

People spray and don't care
That we will die
If this garden isn't shared.
Ladybirds, beetles, ants and bees,
Tiny insects all of these.

Don't squash us,
We do some good.
We eat the bugs that eat your food.
Lettuce, cabbage and apple too,
In the garden for me and you.

EMILY LAMBERT   AGE 5   BARTON ST. DAVID, SOMERSET

Jack's Great Escape

Jack was a field-mouse who lived in a small
hole with his family.

One night when he was having a last minute
walk before he went to bed he bumped into
something.

When he turned round he found he was
trapped inside something. He could not see
what it was and he was so tired he fell asleep
inside it. In the morning he found what it was.
Jack had walked into a bottle. He tried
desperately to find a way out but his eyes were
so full of tears it was useless. Jack was very
thirsty. Then all of a sudden he felt himself
rolling and twisting and then he was free. The
bottle had crashed into a stone. Then Jack
scuttled home.

Not all field-mice are as lucky as Jack was and die of hunger. It is not just field-mice that die because of our litter.

Every bit of rubbish people drop endangers animals' lives.

EMMA DIXON   AGE 10   PLYMOUTH, DEVON

A Sad Mouse's Tale

I'm a poor little mouse lost from my house,
What rotten luck in a bottle I'm stuck,
I have no voice so I can't state my choice,
I just sit down and stare at the ground,
Soon the rain will come down,
Then I will drown.

So wherever you roam,
Please take your bottles home,
And your cans too,
Thank you!

SARAH E. TAYLER   AGE 14   BRAUNSTONE, LEICESTER

The Creature in Our Loft

At the beginning of December we started hearing scuffling in our loft. My mum thought it was my brother running up and down in the middle of the night, but it wasn't. Could it be mice? No, the footsteps were too loud. What could it be? One day my mum went to get some biscuits which she had stored for Christmas in the landing cupboard. Half the packet was gone and there was a nest made in an old woollen blanket. We also found some droppings which were too big for a mouse. We thought it could be a rat or a squirrel. Then we found a hole in the floor-boards in my bedroom. I was beginning to get worried!

We live in a chalet-style house, so there is a loft running along the side of my bedroom. When we looked in my loft, there was a lot of damage. An eaten Red Riding Hood, a deflated Jemima Puddleduck, which was once full with stuffing, and a nibbled Barbie. It had even chewed up a Boglin which looked like something from Nightmare on Elm Street. We called the Pied Piper Pest Control and they said it could be a rat, a squirrel or an edible dormouse. They told us to do the apple test. We had to put down some apple for it and if the apple disappeared it was likely to be an edible dormouse. The next day the apple was gone. It must be an edible dormouse!

At Christmas my grandparents came to stay and my grandma got really annoyed. She said next time she came she hoped we'd have got rid of it. She couldn't stand it running up and down in the loft behind her head and banging. A friend of my mum's lent us a humane trap, because edible dormice are protected. The dormouse must be clever though; it can run in and get the food without getting caught.

Edible dormice were introduced into the country by Lord Rothschild at the turn of the century. He brought them from Europe to his estate in Tring. The edible dormice, or Glis Glis as they are called, escaped, and over the years have spread. They are found in the Oxfordshire/Buckinghamshire area. They are about 6in. long, silvery-grey in colour and look like small chinchillas. Glis Glis were a delicacy in Roman times and were fattened up with walnuts for banquets. The lady from the Pied Piper Pest Control phoned up the Ministry of Agriculture and the man she spoke to hadn't even heard of an edible dormouse.

We have been feeding it regularly with nuts and apples and it's still there. We are dying to see it, but is it really a Glis? We know it likes nuts, we know it likes apples; but we haven't seen it . . . yet!

CHLOË LAFFERTY   AGED 12   CHINNOR, OXON.

6

BIRDS, BATS, BEES AND BUTTERFLIES

I was a graceful cormorant
Swimming in the sea
But one day there was a war
And now look at me

1ST PRIZEWINNER – 8s, 9s and 10s

KATIE PERKINS   AGE 10   LEDBURY, HEREFORDS.

The Threat of Death! – Wild Bird Trade

Two out of four birds die just getting to our pet shops! Parrots are one of the many wild birds that are affected by this horrible trade. Macaws are dying out just because we want to have them in our living-rooms! If you were going to a pet shop you would probably see one macaw or one parrot. They were the lucky ones, most of their friends will have died on the journey. We care for the birds in our garden. Why can't we care for the other birds throughout the world by not buying them and encouraging the people who sell them to stop buying them from the traders.

Remember: what would you prefer to see, a trader with lots of money and the wild birds dead or a trader who has lost his job and the wild birds saved? If you do have a wild bird, anyway, then treat it carefully. Let it have a good life and don't buy another one when it dies. Birds are not the only animals under this threat.

THE THREAT OF DEATH !

SUSIE MACKENZIE   AGE 9   NEWPORT, GWENT

Bird-search

F	R	T	N	A	R	O	M	R	O	C	A
A	E	G	Q	L	S	T	X	I	M	B	R
E	H	C	U	P	L	V	P	S	C	T	C
Z	C	S	W	I	R	U	E	Y	U	A	I
I	T	N	P	D	L	Q	G	R	O	R	I
G	A	N	N	E	T	L	N	A	E	G	C
X	C	B	A	H	B	S	E	P	E	S	T
F	R	G	S	I	T	C	I	M	L	S	E
O	E	D	U	O	A	P	R	J	O	F	R
M	T	C	N	J	D	O	U	N	Q	T	N
R	S	E	R	N	M	P	P	K	Z	Y	C
S	Y	R	A	Z	O	R	B	I	L	L	D
T	O	S	C	L	K	N	I	F	F	U	P

Puffin   Guillemot   Sandpiper
Turnstone   Oyster-catcher   Sea-gull
Arctic tern   Gannet
Razor-bill   Cormorant

Answers on page 156

Answers on page 156

RUTH WHITE   AGE 13   CHILWELL, NOTTINGHAM

Recipe for Bird-cake

Here's a tasty treat you can make. All the birds
love a bit of bird-cake. You won't need
vegetables, you won't need meat. Just melt
some fat on a gentle heat. When it's melted
add some peanuts, and as you do, add a few
raisins and some breadcrumbs too. Other
household scraps like apples, carrot and cheese
can be added now, then when you've added
these pour the mixture slowly into a yoghurt
pot. Then leave it to cool off somewhere where
it isn't hot. When it's hardened take some
scissors and cut the pot away. Then make a
loop with some string and thread it through
the cake. Ask an adult to help you hang the
bird-cake from a hook.

MARGARET ROSE   AGE 11   SUTTON COLDFIELD,
W. MIDLANDS

The Wounded Thrush

One Sunday last summer we heard a loud noise
as something hit our kitchen window. I rushed
outside and found a thrush lying very still on
the ground. Mummy picked it up. It was alive
but it had hurt its wing and was frightened.
We got some hay and made a little nest and
set the thrush on it and placed it in a sunny
spot. Now and again I went to look at it to see
if it was better. Much later it flew away.

1ST RESERVE – 7s and under
JOANNA RITCHIE   AGE 7   COMBER, CO. DOWN,
N. IRELAND

JONATHAN BENTLEY   AGE 14   WERRINTTON,
STOKE-ON-TRENT

Little Owl

This is a true story about a baby owl.

In May 1987 we found a baby owl up in our field, at first we thought it was a bundle of fluff, but then we realized it was a baby owl.

We left it for 24 hours and then came back to it, but it was still there. We read in a book about owls and what they looked like; this baby owl was a Little Owl and they nest in trees, but he fell out. There were no parent birds feeding him, so we took him home and put him in my dad's shed. We made a nest in a wooden box, then we decided to call him Plop. Plop's bedding was black fleece which is nice and soft and warm, it also acts as a mother or father so Plop could snuggle up to it. He liked to cuddle up to our cats because they were nice and warm and they were black like his bed, the cats didn't like it and tried to get away.

We fed him on raw mincemeat, tinned cat food, raw chicken wrapped in feathers, and fresh dead shrews which the cat brought in; Plop ate the shrews whole. We wrapped the chicken in feathers so he could digest his food properly, and produce pellets.

Plop liked being held and he sat on our shoulders and nibbled our ears. His feathers changed from fluff to proper adult feathers, his tail feathers grew as well.

When he started flying we put him outside and he used to sit on the fence, if we whistled and put out our arm he used to swoop down and land on it. After this we put his house outside, so he was free to come and go. Once he was able to peck worms, we fed him in a certain place with shrews and other things, then started to reduce the food so he had to fend for himself.

Then one day he flew off, but we still hear his call around.

RUTH GARDNER   AGE 13   CHESSELL, ISLE OF WIGHT

Young owls often leave their nests before they can fly, so it is quite possible that Plop was not abandoned. Fortunately, the story has a happy ending, but many owls and other birds which are 'rescued' either die or become dependent on humans. If you find a young bird you should leave it alone. (Ed.)

Bird Ringing

I am the youngest member of the North West Norfolk bird Ringing Group (NWNRG), a group consisting of eight people formed in 1990. The group operates at several sites including Burnham Market, Snettisham Coastal Park and Holme Dunes Norfolk Naturalist Trust Nature Reserve.

The birds are ringed and details are recorded consisting of weight, wing-length, fat, age and sex. There are various different ring sizes for the biggest to the smallest bird. All the details will go to the British Trust for Ornithology (BTO). The information helps us to find out where the birds migrate to, where the birds live and hunt, and what they eat. This helps us to find out where the trouble spots are and if their food is contaminated or becoming scarce.

One major problem is theft of eggs. Some eggs can reach thousands of pounds on the black market. At Holme Nature Reserve I act as a voluntary warden, guarding the tern and oyster-catcher nests during the breeding season, day and night. Natural predators are another problem (like grey squirrels and magpies), raiding nests, killing young birds and smashing eggs.

It is not all easy work, most days I have to get up at 4.00 a.m. to get out and set up the mist-nets or traps to catch the birds. Mist-nets are large small-mesh nets 40 or 50 feet long, held up by poles either end. Also a lot of hard work goes into cutting mist-net rides and management of ringing sites, like cutting back trees or planting them. Most days it is natural discoveries we make but the other day we found a mortar bomb cutting a mist-net ride.

If you ever see a ring on a bird try to get the number on the ring. If, unfortunately, the bird is dead, take the ring off and send it to:

> BTO
> The Nunnery
> Thetford
> Norfolk
> IP24 2PU

with the species, if you can identify the bird; but never disturb a bird or walk up to a bird on its nest.

RICHARD LINES   AGE 13   WALTHAM ABBEY, ESSEX

Kiwi

Kenny the kiwi
comes out at night.
He has a long beak
and does not like the light.

ANDREW DOUGLAS   AGE 5   DENNY, SCOTLAND

Penguin Pandemonium

There are 18 different kinds of penguins!
  Penguins cannot fly; they use their tiny
wings as flippers to propel them through the
water.
  Did you know the male Emperor penguin
starves for 64 days whilst incubating its only
egg?

The Emperor penguin is the largest of the penguins, measuring 1.2m. when fully grown.

Penguins' short and shiny feathers give them a waterproof and thermal layer protecting them from icy Antarctic waters.

The little Blue penguin is the smallest of the penguins at only 40cm. tall; it is 1580cm. smaller than the Emperor penguin.

This penguin is called the Chinstrap penguin because of a bold black stripe under its chin.

The Galapagos penguin lives the furthest north, almost on the Equator.

RUTH NEWTON   AGE 14   BASLOW, DERBYS.

The Truth of the Dodos

Let's get one thing clear from the beginning. We, the race of dodos, are anything but stupid. I can say for certain that we're a far sight

cleverer than you apes. Well, I mean all we do
is welcome you humans peacefully and what
do you do? Hit us on the head with clubs and
eat us! We soon realized that peaceful
coexistence was out of the question and, not
being violent or vengeful (another show of
intelligence), we left.

We left in what you'd call spaceships, but
we are still concerned about the welfare of
what we called Old Nest. We make secret visits
occasionally, hence some of your UFO
sightings. We had hoped that our 'extinction'
would instil a sense of responsibility in you.
We were wrong . . . you didn't get better –
you got worse!

When we lived on Old Nest, I mean Earth,
there were so many species of animals that
some joked there was a star for each one (I
wonder if that's why Sirius is called the dog-
star?). That's no longer the case is it? You
humans, with your brilliant inventions, made
sure of that. You invented pesticides which,
when discovered to do more damage to the
environment than intended, are still used
regardless. In fact, most cases of mistreatment
of this, your and our world, centre on your
greed and want of power.

I, Qwark, have been entrusted with the task
of trying to alert you to your plight. In writing
this I risk our race's secrecy about our
existence, but that doesn't matter, we're out of
your reach. Besides, as far as you're concerned
we don't exist. I can see you reading this now

thinking *Dodos are extinct. Some child with a good imagination is just trying to tell us to be more friendly to animals.* Then, probably, you'll go out and buy something cruelly tested on a helpless creature. All well and good as far as we dodos are concerned; we're long gone. But please don't make it so with other animals. Read this and learn, not laugh, because if you don't do something soon, you might be the last animal left. Think and act soon for the dodos' sake.

DANIEL WILLIAMS   AGE 13   WEST BRIDGFORD,
NOTTINGHAM

Your Help is Needed!

The peregrine falcon, the bird that graces the air of the coastlines of Britain, defied all prediction that it would become extinct after the Second World War.

War broke out in 1939 and army divisions would send messages to each other to coincide attacks on the enemy. But how did they send such messages? There were no telephones in use, so how? By pigeon, of course. The pigeon would fly with messages tied to its leg. So how, you ask, does this affect the peregrine? Well, the peregrine's favourite food is, you guessed it, pigeon; and it would attack the carrier pigeon like any other. So the order was put out to soldiers to shoot any peregrine they saw. By the end of the War, peregrines, once common birds, were now nearly wiped out. So over the next years it had a hard task in front of it to avoid extinction.

But peregrines then had other obstacles: egg collectors, poisons and pesticides, and bird snatchers, who snatch young chicks, rear them and sell them to falconers for up to £1000. But this falcon fought on (people became aware of the plight of this bird and it became protected). Their population then started to grow, with fines for anyone who was caught hurting them. Now these falcons, though still rare, once again grace the air with their presence.

But there are others like barn-owls, red kites and golden eagles, to name a few, which aren't so lucky. But you can change that, because the future of these birds is up to you!

ROSS HODDINOTT   AGE 13   BUDE, CORNWALL

Puffins Matter

Stout Puffins
Bobbing on the sea,
Clowning on the cliff-tops
Searching for the sand-eels.
Fishermen have visited and
Caught the silver shoals of sand-eels.
Left the Puffins without food,
So the colonies grow smaller.
Soon, if we don't change our ways,
Instead of Puffin – NOTHING.

FLEUR MOSELEY   AGE 11   IPSWICH, SUFFOLK

The World Needs Bats

1. A vampire bat's saliva can be used to make medicine to help people with heart disease.
2. Bats eat fruit then they sprinkle the seeds on the ground making new plants grow in the rain forest.
3. Bats eat the insects that destroy the rain forest, helping it to grow.
4. Some people hunt bats and in some places bats are served as food but I do not like it. The world needs bats.

MATTHEW VINEY   AGE 7   SELLY PARK, BIRMINGHAM

Bats

Over many years bats have had bad publicity carried by stories, myths and legends. One such story is that of Dracula, which is set in Transylvania and was based on old tales of vampire bats. It is true that they do suck blood from other animals but they only take a little bit and the animals don't even notice. But these bats don't even live in Britain; they are South American.

Most bats are small and only eat fruit or insects. The female bats and their babies live in lofts. Bats are very clean animals, but there is always some oil coming off their fur, so that means there may be oily bits on your wall. Bats only have a baby every two years so that means there isn't a lot to start with. A bat lives for about thirty years, so a female only has about fifteen babies in her life.

Bats are being killed just because of false stories. Now some people are helping bats by making them nests in trees, letting them stay in their lofts and their houses. I hope some day bats and humans will live in peace.

SARAH HARRIS   AGE 11   NEWTOWNARDS, CO. DOWN,
N. IRELAND

Bats for Dinner!

One day when I was getting the potatoes out of the sack for dinner I felt a little soft furry ball instead of a hard potato. When it moved I SCREAMED and Mammy came out to see what was the matter. It was a bat! We carefully checked if it was hurt but it appeared quite well even though it had been taken from the farmer's shed to our home inside a potato sack.

I think it may have got into the sack during the night before the sack was tied.

My family and I stroked its soft velvet coat gently and saw its tiny little eyes. Daddy decided it would be best to leave it in an open shed during the night. When we checked the shed in the morning the bat was gone and we were all happy the little bat was free again.

I prefer potatoes for dinner!

MARIA MCGILL   AGE 7   BALLYMONEY, CO. ANTRIM,
N. IRELAND

Bats

We came silently out of the dark
Like creatures from a half-forgotten dream
Victims of cruel myth and superstition
For blind we are not
Nor entangle in long hair do we
We're crucial to the world
Yet endangered we've become.

Evening comes
We leave the caves
Travelling along restricted paths of ultrasound
Forming one continuous flickering ribbon
We emerge from the cave mouth
Thousands to a minute
A stream of black bodies
Hurtling out over the forest canopy
To begin the night's hunt
Some of us poor creatures

This night are at death's door
As we fly searching for edible insects
Mosquitoes, crickets and flies.

Plastic mesh draped over the country
Lying in wait for us to come
Now here we are
Entangled in this man-trap
Netting holding our wings
No hope of freedom
Mournfully others will fly unsuspecting
To this cruel fate.

But I have a dream
One never to be fulfilled
I have a dream
That I will salvage my brothers, sisters and
   cousins
From the table of delicacies
Enjoyed by mankind
At the expense of 'our' lives and kind
And for what?

ANGELA TUCKER   AGE 14   EDGMOND, SHROPSHIRE

I am a bumble-bee
And you can't replace me
To pollinate the flowers
Would take you many many hours
So please take care of us
You would really miss our buzz.

SARAH HOLT   AGE 7   ALTRINCHAM, CHESHIRE

Butterfly, butterfly
high up in the sky
I hope you never get polluted or die.

KATIE FAULKNER   AGE 5   BANCROFT, MILTON KEYNES

I met a butterfly
It fluttered by
Outside in the garden on its way home
Pretty yellow wings shining in the sun.

MATTHEW PENDLE   AGE 5   WIVENHOE, ESSEX

7

RAIN FOREST AT RISK

Rain Forests

The tropical rain forests are vast, steaming
jungles, teeming with about half of the world's
animal and plant species.

Bananas, coffee, chocolate and nuts come
from the rain forest. They appear so vast and
so strong, but cutting through even a small
part of the rain forest can destroy a lot more.
The bright sun and stormy winds attack the
plants that are not used to the harsh
conditions. Animals and birds are threatened if
their environment is disturbed and are in
danger of extinction. There is about one

species of animal or plant which becomes extinct every day.

The animal responsible for the destruction of the rain forest is, of course, the one called 'man'. He uses the rain forest to chop down valuable timber like mahogany, teak and ebony or to clear space for grazing animals. The animals and plants pay the consequences for man's greed.

ANIL CHUDASAMA   AGE 14   MAIDSTONE, KENT

Rain Forest Sandwich

Ingredients

Brown bread
Margarine
Pickle is the soil
Lettuce is the grass
Watercress is the vines
Cheese is the trunks of trees
Cucumber is the tops of trees
Tomatoes are flowers

First spread brown bread with margarine and then with pickle; lay lettuce on top and then watercress. Cut cheese into stems and lay like trunks; put the cucumber on top of the cheese and then slice tomatoes and put on to sandwich. It can have another slice of bread on top of it or it can be an open sandwich.

ALASTAIR CRACKNELL   AGE 7   WINGHAM, KENT

Rain Forest Wordsearch

Rain forests provide a home for 50% of the world's species and yet destruction of them has increased by a huge 90% in the past ten years.

M	H	U	M	M	I	N	G	B	I	R	D	Y
O	S	T	O	R	T	O	I	S	E	Z	H	A
N	R	O	F	J	P	D	H	M	B	G	T	N
K	Z	U	U	C	I	A	U	A	H	S	O	T
E	A	C	R	Y	X	L	R	P	E	O	L	E
Y	C	A	P	J	C	E	K	R	M	T	S	A
S	W	N	G	A	K	M	B	T	O	B	K	T
M	A	C	A	W	S	U	S	P	M	T	U	E
N	B	U	T	T	E	R	F	L	Y	E	S	R
F	O	P	L	E	D	T	U	R	T	L	E	S

Find these endangered species in the grid above:

Macaw   Humming-bird
Toucan   Tortoise
Butterfly   Sloth
Turtle   Monkey
Ant-eater   Lemur
Parrot

Answers on page 156

SALLY DENNIS   AGE 15   REDRUTH, CORNWALL

The Rain Forest

THE RAINFOREST WAS BEING CUT DOWN
RAPIDLY BY HUMANS, LEAVING THE ANIMALS
HOMELESS.

MEANWHILE, PRESIDENT BYRD WAS READING ABOUT
THE ANIMAL'S PLIGHT, WHEN HE HAD AN IDEA ....

THE ANIMALS HELD A MEETING, BUT COULD DO
NOTHING.

HE SENT BIRDS TO DROP SUPPLIES OF FOOD TO THE ANIMALS.

THE ANIMALS HAD ENOUGH FOOD NOW, BUT
THEY COULD STILL NOT DO ANYTHING
ABOUT THE DESTRUCTION OF THEIR HOMES.
ONLY HUMANS HAD THE POWER TO
SAVE THEM NOW, BUT HUMANS WERE
THE ONES WHO WERE KILLING THEM.
WHAT COULD THEY DO? BUT SOME
HUMANS DID CARE. THEY WANTED TO
HELP – AND DID.

THE WORKMEN WERE DEFEATED. THEY LEFT, AND THE ANIMALS AND RAINFOREST WERE SAVED.

CLAIRE MORIARTY   AGE 13   CHANDLERS FORD, HANTS.

Progress

Long, long ago, in the days of the great forest,
the world was very different. If maps existed
then, they would show no cities and no
farmland because such things were not around.
Long, long ago the great oak was tall and
strong, great in number and bird-song filled
its upper branches. Woodland streams ran
freely through the trees, and pure, clean water
was the usual thing. Long, long ago every
living thing had its fair share in the world,
and everything that was taken was given back.
Every creature and every plant helped support
the environment which it, along with so many
others, depended on. People were *part* of this.

Deep in the darkest darkness of the life tree,
in the heart of the forest, the all-seeing silent
one, who flies by night only, could sleep in
peace. He was content, but he always feared
something . . . something which he could not
put a finger on, but was there.

The years passed through grim, dormant
winter, through bright, vibrant spring, long,
relaxed summer, and breezy, colourful autumn.
And no matter how hard the winter there was
always life at the end. But one year, the clouds
rolled darker every day, and the autumn storms
lashed the slender beech trunks more savagely.
The silent one huddled deeper into his
darkness and thought harder, feared worse.
This would be the hardest winter yet, the
winter of progress. That winter, the two-legged

hunting one's ideas were changing; they were not satisfied with their equal share, give and take existence; they wanted more.

The winter of progress has lasted, for today we still have the sophisticated tools of the human race. The idea that people have to be dependent on other people to live properly. After all, you can't have a TV, video, car, even food, if no one makes and sells it. Long ago, if any creature was injured or old, it had to cope as best as it could; not so now. Long ago you had to find your own survival or die. Long ago people did not need bankers, political parties, produce companies to keep them alive, because nature provided them with all their needs. We have tried to fill all the niches intended for others, and surely that cannot be right. Nature's great experiment has failed; one more gifted species cannot live by the given guidelines, it always has to step over them. Every experiment that goes wrong must be corrected or something disastrous may happen.

The winter may be long and hard but at the end there will be a spring. Far, far away from the comforts of civilization, beyond the windswept moors, there is a last forest, and in it, the darkest, most ancient forces are growing in strength. One day they will go to war and they will win and the silent one will sleep peacefully again. Until then, we must do what we can to help. And if you don't understand, then go to a town and be a typical human. Spend some money, eat some bought food, go to the pictures. Afterwards, sit down on a busy high street, and watch and listen and think.

Later, take a walk in a wood, or on a moor and watch, and listen and think hard. Then you might understand better.

JAMIE HUDSON   AGE 14   BEVERLEY, N. HUMBERSIDE

8

WHY SHOULD ANIMALS SUFFER?

Forget the rain forest for a moment. Look in the fridge and look at the eggs in there. They're probably not free-range are they? If they are not free-range it most likely means they come from a battery farm. In a battery farm they are produced in a terrible way. The chickens are cooped up in tiny cages (about five birds in each cage) and are forced to lay eggs for your breakfast. Most of the chickens die in the cages and are left there. Millions of chickens die every month, so you can have eggs for breakfast; so think on that next time you have an egg that is not free-range.

Next, go up to your mum's make-up drawer and have a quick look on the labels and you might find a little picture of a rabbit to show that it's not tested on animals, or there might be words instead of a picture. Make-up and cosmetics tested on animals may also contain animal produce. White rabbits have perfumes and shampoos dropped into their eyes (also known as a draize test). For testing lipstick and cosmetics that go near the mouth, they mostly use the LD50 test (LD = lethal dose); a group of animals (usually rats or mice) are force-fed large quantities of a substance, such as lipstick, until 50% die. Cruelty-free make-up may cost a lot of money, but it's worth it to know that there aren't any animals suffering just because you want to look beautiful.

Next, go to your mum's or your sister's wardrobe and see if there's a leather handbag or purse. It may be fake leather and if it is she scores 10 out of 10. If it's not it could be made out of crocodile skin (or any other animal). Crocodiles suffer terrible cruelty when killed for their skin. They're killed at only four years old, for skins that are made into handbags. Sometimes the crocodiles are skinned alive because it's thought to produce higher quality leather.

Next, go to the fridge in the kitchen. Look at the meat. The ham and the beef, the hamburgers and the chicken. Let's start with the hamburgers. Large amounts of rain forest are being chopped down so that grass can grow there and cattle can graze on it and be fattened up for slaughter. Now for the rest of the meat.

Most people say meat is good for you. But I
think that is only if it's organic meat. (That
means the meat hasn't any chemicals in it.)
But organic meat isn't very common. Most of
the meat in the shops is filled with chemicals
to fatten it up, and when the animals have
been killed, the chemicals stay in the meat.
Most of that is passed on to us, and sometimes
makes us ill. More people that eat meat die of
heart disease than vegetarians. So if you
become vegetarian, you will not only save
yourself, you might also save a few animals.
Half the world's population is now vegetarian,
but it's not enough! Why don't *you* try going
vegetarian for a week and see how
you like it. I have been a vegetarian
for nearly seven years and I feel a lot
healthier than I did seven years ago.

3RD PRIZEWINNER – 11s to 15s

REBECCA GULLIVER   AGE 13   MARLBOROUGH, WILTS.

Tommy

Hi, my name is Tommy; I'm two years old and
I'm a beagle dog. I bet you're thinking that
I'm a happy little dog with a nice home and
loving owners? Well you're quite wrong. I try
to be as happy as possible, but it's not easy
when you have a raw, shaved back, covered
with open sores where you've had cream rubbed
on to it, so that humans can be safe and use it.
My friends the rats are treated in a similar way.

They are fed sun-tan lotion which makes their fur go orange, makes them very ill and lifeless. Other animals in this place are sick or bleeding from the effects of drugs. Some are poisoned with pesticides or force-fed toothpastes.

Got to go, the humans are going to rub some more cream on my back.

HELEN COURTNEY   AGE 10   WAKEFIELD, W. YORKS.

Animal Experimentations

Should animals be used to test cosmetics?

In 1989 over 12,000 animals, including rabbits, guinea-pigs, mice and rats were used to test cosmetics, toiletries and their ingredients in British laboratories.

Some people might be confused and not know what is meant by animal experimentation. It is when animals are used to test either cosmetics or medicine, to be used by humans. I am not writing about medical experiments, but cosmetics are not necessary to human life, so why should animals suffer in the most inhuman ways to produce a product to make human beings look good?

Next time you go to buy some cosmetics or washing powders, check the label and make sure they are not tested on animals, because if enough people stop buying these goods then unnecessary animal experimentations should stop.

I hope you now think the answer to the question above is yes, animal experimentations should be stopped.

For more information please write to:

Choose Cruelty Free
BUAV
15a Crane Grove
Islington
London N7 8LB

LUCY FREEMAN   AGE 15   CLAVERLEY, W. MIDLANDS

Herbal Beauty

Do you think animals should suffer? They are tested on just for us; it is cruel and unnecessary. But here is an idea that is only tested on you.

HERBAL VINEGAR

Ingredients

Dried lavender flowers
Dried rose petals
Cider vinegar

Method

Put all the ingredients in a wide-necked bottle. Shake well and leave on a sunny window-sill for about four weeks shaking every day; then drain all the herbs. Splash a little on your face every day.

HANNAH MARSHALL   AGE 10   COLSTERWORTH, LINCS.

Animal Thoughts

All us animals think it is true,
We should have rights just like you.
All we want is to be loved,
Not tested on, poked or shoved.
We are locked in cages, put in pain,
Do you humans have no shame?
We think the scientists are mean,
They test on us until we scream.
They put samples in our eyes,
This is the truth, we tell no lies.
Every day we are full of dread,
All we may as well be is dead.
Why do you treat us like you do?
What have we ever done to you?
Why let this happen; can't you see,
If you help us we could be free.

ALEX STOTHARD   AGE 13   NORWICH, NORFOLK

9

ANIMAL FASHION

My Aunty Just Loves Fur

My aunty always dresses in fur,
And shoes of crocodile skin,
With a racoon's tail, she'll bind her hair,
And a snake-skin bag to put her purse in.

She'll go to great extent,
To make sure she looks to her delight.
I try to tell her fur is wrong,
But she argues it is right.

But animals are living creatures,
Who share this world with us too.
'Who cares?' she laughs. 'Don't make a fuss.
You don't want me to walk naked, do you?'

'No Aunty, but –'
'That's fine then. Yes that's right.'
'But –' 'Don't argue child,
I don't want to fight!'

We continued to debate,
About the cause for my upset,
So she agreed to look for a substitute,
And the argument, at a standstill, came to rest.

I took her to a clothes shop,
She saw a coat she liked.
The coat was made of fake fur,
And at a reasonable price.

She said to the man, 'I'll take it!'
'Anything else, madam?' he asked.
'No, thank you, sir, I think it'll fit.
It's the nicest coat I've had!'

When we got home, she tried on the coat,
And looked in the mirror with pride,
'So there is an alternative to fur and slaughter,
And it looks just as good,' she cried.

DON'T BE A WALKING, TALKING ANIMAL DESTROYER!

NATASHA KELLY   AGE 14   HANDSWORTH WOOD,

BIRMINGHAM

What I Think About Fur

Fur looks much better on an animal than on a person.

Tens of millions of animals a year, unfortunate enough to have been born with beautiful fur coats, are trapped and killed or imprisoned in fur factories for a fraction of their natural lifespans. Their skins are ripped from their bodies to satisfy ignorant vanity and to make fat profits for greedy people. Each year 100 million animals are slaughtered for their coats, that's 8,000 every hour, or 133 every minute! But whichever way you like to put it, animals are being murdered for humans, they are being murdered for us.

WHAT CAN YOU DO ABOUT IT?

There are 80 fur farms in Great Britain, so find out if there's a fur farm in your area and ask your local newspaper to write a story about it. You might be surprised to hear about how many other people from your area will object to a fur farm being in their district. If that doesn't help, write to your local MP. Encourage your family and friends to write too. By creating a fuss, you're more likely to get action out of the politicians. ANIMALS MATTER.

CATHERINE DUCKETT   AGE 13   CHELMSFORD, ESSEX

ALEXANDRA LYMER   AGE 13   STOKE-ON-TRENT, STAFFS.

An Open Letter From a Crocodile

To anybody who'll listen,

I wish we didn't have such a bad reputation among men, because then we might have a better chance of human support in recovering our numbers to a level safe from extinction. We're known to be violent, but when we're attacked by poachers, our natural reaction is to fight for our lives, even if we know we've only got a slim chance of survival anyway. And I'm sure that poachers would fight back if they were hunted!

Our most valuable skins are those above 6ft. long. But Nile crocodiles can only breed at 9ft. or over. Less and less eggs are laid every year, and even once they have been laid there is a risk of them being washed into the water by power launches. And our area of territory is restricted by fishermen's nets all the way across the river.

The few men that want to prevent our becoming extinct say that the best way to increase our numbers is to farm us and make the shooting of crocodiles and the trading of our skins legal, and I must say that I don't much like the sound of it. Even so, something has certainly got to be done, and whatever it is, we need your help urgently.

Thank you for listening,
The Crocodilians

TAMSIN SCOTT   AGE 13   EAST MALLING, KENT

The Crocodile

There was a crocodile called Chris,
Who said, 'I've had enough of this,
Those humans who think they can use
My skin to make a pair of shoes!'
So he thought of a cunning plan
And gobbled up a passing man
And with the skin he didn't eat
He made some trainers for his feet!

DANIELLE HART   AGE 11   CHINGFORD, ESSEX

I don't want to get hurt, I don't want to be
some shoes; I don't want to be a croc-skin
bag, it really gives me the blues. Crocodiles
have their rights too, you really make me sad.
How would you like to be a
HUMAN-SKIN BAG.

BRYONY MACKENZIE   AGE 12   HOLMFIRTH, W. YORKS.

JOSHUA WATSON   AGE 5   CHEW STOKE, BRISTOL

10

ONE SMALL STEP FOR VEGETARIANISM

The Animal Conference – and the events of this meeting . . .

After careful contemplation
And much deliberation,
Came this stunning revelation
From the spokesman for the lions.

'There has been some indignation
At our grisly occupation
Of eating our relations
Such as zebras and gnus.

'So to end this consternation,
We propose the conservation
Of the zebra population
(Not forgetting the gnus).

'We'll eat red meat in moderation,
Fill up with vegetation,
And resist the great temptation
To eat you between meals.'

This speech met with jubilation
And a well deserved ovation
From each creature of each nation,
Especially the gnus.

But amidst all the elation
Came a giraffe's vociferation,
'We'll all die of starvation,
If the lions eat our leaves!'

'Not a chance with our creation,'
Was the lion's exclamation,
'Of a giant yam plantation
In Sudan!'

And so began the preservation
Of the coming generations
And the massive importation
Of dried figs.

One small step for vegetarianism,
And one giant leap for the gnu.

2ND PRIZEWINNER – 11s to 15s

PAUL THURTLE   AGE 14   ROTHERHAM, S. YORKS.

Safety Note

Make sure you have an adult with you when you are trying out any of the following recipes. (Ed.)

How To Make a Vegetarian Pizza

(This is a recipe for an animal-friendly pizza)

For the dough

4oz of self-raising flour
1oz of butter or fat
Pinch of salt
1 egg
Milk to mix

For the topping

1 tbsp oil
2 small onions
1–2 tbsp tomato purée
14oz (400g) tin of tomatoes
2 tsp of mixed herbs
6oz (130g) of sweet corn
6oz (175g) of cheddar cheese
4 mushrooms
Some butter

Making the dough

1. Rub the flour and fat together to make breadcrumbs.
2. Add salt and the egg and stir.
3. Knead into dough (add milk if necessary).
4. Roll out into a circular shape, about 1 cm. thick.

Making the topping

1. Mix the tomato purée, the tin of tomatoes and the herbs together into a thick sauce.
2. Heat the oil in a saucepan and gently fry the onions which have been peeled and finely chopped for 10–15 minutes.
3. Mix the onions into the sauce.
4. Spread it over the top of the pizza base.
5. Cover it with the sweet corn (which has boiled for about 5 minutes on a high heat).
6. Grate the cheese and sprinkle on top of the sweet corn.
7. Slice the mushrooms in half and fry them in the butter on a gentle heat for about 5 minutes and place on the top of the pizza. Cook in an oven (400 °F or 200 °C, Gas 6) for 20–30 minutes.

REBECCA LEVERINGTON   AGE 12   SAFFRON WALDEN,
ESSEX

Special Vegetable Layer

Ingredients

1lb (450g) potatoes
½ cauliflower
8oz (200g) carrots
2oz (50g) mushrooms
4oz (100g) green beans, tinned or frozen
4oz (100g) cheddar cheese
2 eggs
½ pint (250ml) milk
Salt and pepper

Method

1. Preheat the oven to 180 °C/350 °F/Gas 4.
2. Peel the potatoes and slice them into rings about ¼″ (5mm.) wide.
3. Wash the cauliflower and break into small florets.
4. Wash, peel and slice the carrots into rings.
5. Wash the mushrooms and slice finely.
6. Grate the cheddar cheese.
7. Put layers of potato, cauliflower, carrot, mushroom, green beans and grated cheese into a buttered casserole dish. Repeat until all the vegetables are used up, finishing with a layer of cheese.
8. Beat the eggs, milk, salt and pepper and pour over the vegetables.
9. Cook for 1½ hours in the oven, until set and golden brown.

CAROLYN HISCOCK   AGE 12   WIMBORNE, DORSET

Vegetable Curry

Vegetables as available, e.g.

Onion – coarsely chopped
4 carrots, diced
4 celery sticks
Small cauliflower broken into florets
Green pepper, seeds removed and sliced into
    rings and cut into 1 cm. pieces
Courgettes, sliced
Tbsp of ground coriander
Tbsp of ground cumin
Tbsp of ground fenugreek
$\frac{1}{2}$ tsp chilli powder
Tsp ground cardamom seeds
3 garlic cloves
2·5 cm. piece of ginger
5 tbsp vegetable oil
300 ml. water
2–3 tbsp lemon
    juice

Fry onion until light brown, add crushed garlic
and finely chopped ginger. In a bowl make a
paste with the ground spices and 2–3
tablespoons of lemon juice. Add paste to
onions and fry for one minute, stirring

continually. Add a few drops of water if mixture sticks. Add carrots, cauliflower and water, bring to the boil and gently simmer. After 10 minutes add rest of vegetables and simmer until tender.

EMMA CATESBY   AGE 11   BILLERICAY, ESSEX

Gregory's Pasties (Vegan)

Pastry

8oz flour
4oz margarine (veg)
Little drop of water

Mix flour and margarine together, add water to make pastry.

Filling

1oz margarine (veg)
1 large onion, chopped
4oz mushrooms, chopped
2oz cabbage, chopped
1 large tin of baked beans
Pinch of pepper and oregano

Cook onion, margarine, cabbage and mushrooms for five minutes in a saucepan and add beans, pepper and oregano. Cool, then make into pasties with the pastry. Cook in oven (400° F, 200° C or Gas 6). Eat with salad and chips.

GREGORY BROOK   AGE 7   LLANTWIT MAJOR,
S. GLAMORGAN

Vegetable and Nut Risotto

This is one of my favourite meals. This amount is enough for me and my two sisters.

Ingredients

Brown rice measured up to 150ml mark in measuring jug
Water measured up to 300 ml mark
1 tbs vegetable oil
1 small onion, chopped
½ vegetable stock cube
1 medium carrot
½ red pepper
2 tbsp sweet corn
2 tbsp peas
2 tbsp cashew nuts
Salt, pepper, herbs to taste

Put oil in a saucepan over low heat. Add onion and cook until soft. Add rice and carrot and stir for a few minutes. Add water and stock cube and simmer gently for 15–20 minutes or until the stock is almost absorbed. Add rest of ingredients, stir and cook for a further 5 minutes. Sometimes we sprinkle cheese on top too.

BEN FISHER   AGE 5   FAVERSHAM, KENT

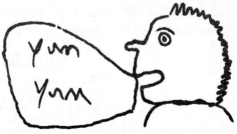

What a Vegetarian Really Thinks

Hello!

I'm a vegetarian! It's not just because I don't really like the taste of meat and fish, but also I am an animal's friend.

Some people think that I can't possibly be eating enough protein but they don't realize how many other sources of protein there are in this world: nuts, peas and beans are all full of protein.

Yet more people think that I should be ill all the time because I don't eat meat. But really I'm just as healthy as any meat-eater!

Perhaps even more people would imagine that when I see people enjoying meat and fish I would feel left out, but that really isn't true. I have seen the conditions in which animals (kept for meat) live in.

In some countries, mainly in Asia, people don't think twice about eating cats and dogs, whereas here in Europe most people would say 'yuk' to this. Of course, so would I, but to me it is just the same as eating a little lamb or calf.

If anyone is thinking about becoming a vegetarian, providing their family is willing to prepare vegetarian meals for them, I say 'go for it!' After all, I've been a vegetarian since I was one and I'm still alive! And remember – a true animal lover is always a vegetarian.

MADELEINE FROST   AGE 12   WORTH, W. SUSSEX

11

AT THE ZOO

Zoos at this moment in time are very popular
with families, especially with young children.
Lots of people enjoy the zoo for a day-trip
out. Most people only think of zoos as skin
deep; they have never taken a look from behind
the bars. People never even think of how the
animals must feel; as far as they are concerned
they are there to entertain them. We must
STOP and think about how they feel. A lot of
the animals go mad and show very good signs
of it; this may be due to the very small areas
they are given to live in. There are some
groups that are against zoos. Zoocheck – they

are good. Zoos I think should be done away with. They should have types of zoos just for endangered species which, after the numbers have increased, should be set free.

EMMA SHEPPARD   AGE 13   MARKET HARBOROUGH, LEICS.

What Do the Animals Think?

I was climbing through the jungle
When I heard a human shout,
'Look at that gorilla,
We could catch it without doubt!'
Why were they chasing me?
There was nothing I could do.
They put me straight to sleep,
And I woke up in a ZOO!
I was trapped inside a cage
With no trees to climb.
At least the other animals
Could help me pass the time!

Lots of people come and go,
Staring closely at me.
Children look in wonder,
As if there's much to see!
Later I was moved away
By someone that I knew
To a big safari park,
It's much better than the zoo!!

DEAN WILLIAMS   AGE 13   SALTASH, CORNWALL

IF WE CARRY ON PUTTING ANIMALS IN SMALL CAGES
THEY MIGHT ONE DAY START DOING IT TO US

MARIANNE MEDLOCK   AGE 9   EYE, SUFFOLK

The Cruel Zoo

The first cage says 'Chimpanzee',
I stare into gloom, then I see
Two sorrowful eyes staring at me
Saying as plain as plain can be,
'Set me free, set me free!'

I move on from this awful sight
And see a tiger, eyes alight.
His gleaming eyes say, 'I will bite.
Let me out and let me fight.
I will *not* be cooped up tight.'

I've seen this zoo, I've walked about
And every animal throughout

Has said as loud as eyes can shout,
'Let me out! LET ME OUT!
Oh, why won't someone let me out?'

EMMA JONES   AGE 14   LITTLEOVER, DERBY

Zoo Cares?

Is it right, I ask myself, to lock them up like
   criminals
When their only crime is to be born into our
   unkind world?
Are we too busy to stop and think of these
   poor animals
As we stand and watch them caged and bored?

But if they were not here, where would they be?
In forest green, on sprawling plain or
   swimming in the sea.
Living their lives as their lives should be run,
Free and happy under blue skies and warm sun.

But think again, their forests are dying and bare,
Their plains riddled by poachers and haunted
   by death.
Their oceans are polluted, so sad, so unfair
And when we are finished what will they have
   left?

So perhaps it is right to put them in zoos
Until we have learned to restore nature's
   balance,
To stop chopping down trees that we don't
   need to use,
Or killing the seas with our oil and pollutants.

Be thankful, sad, beautiful tiger, bright parrot,
Don't cry, woolly monkey – swing, dance and
  chatter.
Remember that some of us are making an
  effort
Because we believe that the Animals Matter.

STEPHEN PYE   AGE 13   SUTTON, SURREY

Don't Keep Animals in a Cage

CHRISTOPHER SMITH   AGE 4   AYLESFORD, KENT

12

AND HUMANS CALL THIS SPORT!

A Fox's Account of a Foxhunt

I lay low in the undergrowth at the edge of
the woods, sniffing the air for the scent of
danger. A squirrel in the trees above me
dropped a nutshell. At the soft *thud* in the
earth behind me, I spun round, baring my
teeth and holding up my brush. Looking up
and seeing the squirrel, I promptly gave one
last sniff, turned my back on the woods and
trotted at a comfortable pace through the
neighbouring cornfield. I stopped once to sniff

at a field-mouse, when I caught the familiar smell of rabbits. At this I became suddenly stealthy, silently running to the edge of the cornfield and peering out from between the stalks of corn. The rabbit was unaware of my presence, so I pounced and snapped its neck instantly. It made a good meal. I decided the next thing that I caught would be for my wife and cubs.

Five minutes later, as I passed Midler's Wood, I heard the sound every fox dreads. The huntsman's bugle. I turned and ran swiftly, hoping the hounds would not catch my smell, but it was a vain hope. The hounds' bloodthirsty cries from behind me encouraged me to run faster. I jumped over the brook, heading for the heart of where the trees grew close together. I enjoyed the thrill of speed as I leapt over a low stone wall. At the heart of the wood I skilfully dodged through the trees, the leader of the pack of dogs practically breathing down my neck. The rest of the dogs were a distance back, the lead dog being the fittest. I darted round a bramble bush the dog had not seen, and I heard it yelp in pain as it pricked itself on the sharp thorns. The dog, however fast, was not as agile as me, and as I dodged the trees, the dog bashed its head on a large oak and fell unconscious. The rest of the dogs would not chase without their leader, so I turned and headed for my den to rest.

PAUL WALKER   AGE 11   LANCHESTER, DURHAM

NOW YOU KNOW WHAT IT FEELS LIKE!

HELEN GRACE   AGE 15   MALTON, N. YORKS.

A Fox's Diary

Friday 12th April
Dear Diary,
  I am on the run, the hunters are after me,
they want my life, they want to send their dogs
to catch me and tear me limb from limb. I
have heard of this terrible fate happening to
others but I never thought it would happen to
me. Apparently it is supposed to keep down
our numbers, but those silly humans know
nothing; you see, foxes live in groups, but only
one male in that group mates with the
females. When we are hunted, the group
splits up and forms new groups (which

should never have been formed), males mate (which should never have mated) and babies are born (which never should have been born).

I am in a bush to catch my breath and write this diary entry as it may be my last. I can hear the pounding of paws. I must dash. If they get me may I rest in peace and may they drown in guilt . . .

LISA DUELL   AGE 14   SOUTHAMPTON, HANTS.

The Other Way Round

Have you ever thought of it
the other way round
Where the human is the fox
and the fox is the hound?
Safely in our beds
we'd hear the dreaded horn.
We'd have to leave our homes
before the crack of dawn.
Trying all our tactics
to put them off our trail.
No practice, no second chance,
woe betide us if we fail.
The fox would be our enemy,
the one to be most feared.
As a neighbour, a friend,
or a mum just disappeared!
We are on the increase,
getting out of hand.
To cut the numbers, they must hunt us

and we must understand.
But can this be the reason,
or is it just for sport?
For if it *were* the other way round
would *you* like to be caught?

KATE BRYAN   AGE 14   BRAMCOTE, NOTTINGHAM

Badger Baiting

I never used to know why Dad kept the terriers,
I thought they were just the family pets,
Although they didn't live in the house like
   normal dogs,
They lived in the yard, at the back, in a shed.

Every Saturday morning Dad used to take them
From the back of the yard, from the shed
   where they lived,
Out across the fields, Dad laughing, dogs
   yelping,
I thought it was just for a walk, well, that's
   what he said.

And then one day I followed them,
Out across the fields, hiding as I went,
It was then, that day, that I saw them,
Dogs yelping, Dad with a spade in his hand,
   his head bent.

I started yelling, trying to stop them,
By now I knew what they were going to do,
I wanted to shout, 'I hate you Dad,'
But now the badger was out, babies following too.

I ran forward blindly,
I was running for that badger, trying not to
  make a sound,
But now the dogs were on it,
And the sound of police cars filled the nearby
  ground.

Now every Saturday morning I go and see my
  dad,
I know he regrets it, I know that he is sad,
He said he didn't mean to hurt anything, and
  I don't know if that's true,
As it wasn't just that badger he killed, it was
  lots of others too.

JOANNE BALLARD   AGE 13   LOUGHBOROUGH, LEICS.

13

PETS – OUR BEST FRIENDS?

Animals matter because they can help to make you better. My mum is a District Nurse and she sometimes takes our dog, Lady, to work with her and the people can stroke her and it makes them happy. You can also take them for a walk and play games with them and that is good for you. I ride my pony, Bimbo, which is nice and good exercise. It is nice for people to watch animals, it feels good. I love all animals.

LAURA RIDLEY   AGE 6   MATLOCK, DERBYS.

Dear Reader,

I am not your average dog. I see myself as
special because I have a very important job.
I'm a guide-dog for the blind. This, of course,
does not mean I matter more than other
animals, but it does mean I am one of the best
examples of animal and human co-operation.
After all, if we animals did not run the world,
you humans would be extinct by now! I know
I matter because I am the only substitute for
the eyes of the blind person I own. My reward
is the love and affection I receive because he
too knows that 'animals matter'!

Love Couger.
PS   If you see me working, remember not to
distract me; a blind person's safety is in my
hands (I mean paws – it seems I'm becoming
human).

FRANCESCO FERRANDINO   AGE 15   BLACKBURN, LANCS.

PAT Dogs

I have a dog called Henry. He is a four-year-old cocker spaniel. He has won many prizes at dog shows. But he has another very important role. Henry is also a PAT dog. PAT stands for Pro dogs Active Therapy. PAT dogs visit hospitals and nursing homes bringing friendship and pleasure to many people. The PAT dog scheme was first tried out in the Derbyshire area, before being launched nationally in 1983.

People take their dogs to old people's homes because although quite often the pensioners have friends, they miss having dogs or any animals to stroke. Being able to pat and stroke the dogs reminds them of the pets they had. The scheme has been found to have all-round benefits. For instance, a man in hospital had been taking sleeping-tablets for a long time. A PAT dog was brought on to the ward at bedtime each evening, so that the man could stroke the dog till he fell asleep. After a few weeks he did not need sleeping-tablets any more.

Any breed, cross-breed or age of dog can be a PAT dog, but it must have a good temperament and like lots of fuss. It is not just old people's homes PAT dogs visit, they go on children's wards in hospitals and to some mental institutions as well. The PAT dogs do things to raise money for hospitals and charities as well.

PAT dogs is a branch of PRO dogs which is a registered charity. Their motto is 'PRO dogs cares, defends and protects'. PAT dogs take part in sponsored events and they have stands at some big dog shows like Crufts. There are several PAT dog awards you can win such as Tandem PAT Dog Awards. They are nominated for these by the people they visit. There are over 5000 PAT dogs and we still cannot meet the demand. The 5000th registered PAT dog is a cocker spaniel called Ella.

A social care magazine called the work that PAT dogs do 'tail-wagging psychotherapy'. The scheme clearly shows the importance of companion animals to people.

GARY HOWELL   AGE 15   REDDITCH, WORCS.

A Dog is for Life

All alone here I sit
In my home on the street,
Just a stray in the world
With nothing to eat.

I'm all by myself
My only future is to die,
Put to sleep by a needle,
No one there to say goodbye.

I remember a time
(I'll never forget)
When I lived with a family
As their household pet.

Those four kindly people
Played with me each day,
I loved them, they loved me,
Things were perfect in every way.

But then they started to ignore me,
They seemed to forget I was there.
They never gave me food or water,
They simply stopped seeming to care.

One happy day we went for a ride,
I sat with the kids in the back,
When the car stopped, THEY didn't get out,
Just dumped ME on the side of the track.

So I lay there crying and abandoned
As the big car rolled away,
I'd never have given them all that devotion
If I'd known this was the way they'd repay.

So there's something I want you to remember,
A fact that by all should be known;
I'm not just a toy to amuse you,
I have got a life of my own.

(By a little stray doggy!)

JESSICA YUILLE   AGE 13   DROITWICH, WORCS.

Animals Matter

Animals definitely do matter, especially a
certain dog – Shandy. If it wasn't for Shandy,
my dad wouldn't be here today. I'll tell you
what happened.

My dad is a policeman and had a police dog
– a German shepherd (Shandy). One night, my
dad was called out to a very dangerous
burglary. When my dad got there the house
was surrounded with the burglars in it and all
the police outside. The trouble was, the
burglar had a hostage, a three-year-old girl.
The burglar walked out of the house with the
girl in front of him so no one could get to
him. He said that he wanted to talk to just one
unarmed policeman on his own or he'd shoot
the girl. So my dad went with him. The
burglar took him to the alley-way near the
house. The rest of the police had been warned
to stay clear. When they reached the alley, the
burglar immediately pulled out a gun and
pointed it at my dad, saying, 'This'll show the
rest of the police how serious I am.' He pulled
the trigger and the bullet was heading straight
for my dad. It would have hit him if it hadn't
been for Shandy. Shandy had escaped and
followed my dad's scent. He jumped in the
way of the bullet and was very tragically killed.
So my dad owes his life to Shandy. But that is
only my dad's story. I'm sure animals have
saved people's lives plenty of times. Like the
St. Bernard dogs that save people that get
trapped in the snow. Animals definitely do
matter.

SARAH ATKINS   AGE 13   BILLERICAY, ESSEX

Six Ways to be Kind and Not Cruel to Your Pets

1. If for some reason you have to leave your dog in the car when you go out, PLEASE, for your dog's sake, leave the window open slightly. Some dogs have died or become ill or unconscious from being left in a hot, stuffy car for too long.

2. If you have a fish-pond in your garden, put some mesh over it. If the fish in there think the birds can get to it, the fish may die of shock or, if not, become so timid that they hide at the bottom and only come up for food when no one is around.

3. Remember, remember the fifth of November . . . oh, forget all that! What you *really* need to remember is to keep your pets indoors where they will be safe from the loud noises and bright lights of fireworks. They are not used to them and will be scared.

4. Your pet is *not* a soft toy. Pick it up gently and in a sensible way. Do not pick it up by its ears, its tail or by its stomach without supporting its hind legs; you could seriously hurt it.

5. If you have a bird, let it out of its cage every few days so it can stretch its wings. But make sure all windows and doors are shut; your bird may be feeling adventurous!

6. When you go on holiday, be it a weekend, a week, or two, always get somebody to feed and care for your pets. They could become thin, ill, weak or even die.

JENNY WARD   AGE 11   SOLIHULL, W. MIDLANDS

Life in Your Hands

We had been discussing it for ages but it was never a reality. Then one evening we decided. Mum and I were hysterical and I sat with Jimbo for hours. Dad didn't cry then, but I think he did later on that evening. It's unbelievable that in just five seconds an animal can die and you'll never see them again. I loved my cat so much and it came as a big shock. I know it was the right thing to do because Jimbo was ill, but I feel guilty that she couldn't make the decision to die. Even though I cried before we took her to the vet I still couldn't believe she was gone.

When we got to the vet I tried to be brave, but I started crying as we sat in the waiting-room. I had my hand in Jim's basket and she was rubbing her face against it. Whenever I took my hand away she miaowed. I'm sure that she sensed something was wrong because she was acting very strangely.

The vet's door opened and we were called in. Vets must be so used to putting animals down that they don't get emotionally involved. The vet was a nice Australian lady who we've seen before. I opened the basket and Jim looked up at me. She climbed out of the basket and the vet put a strap on her leg. Jim hated that and she managed to hiss and growl even though she was so weak. I stroked her head and cried, but I did need to be there with her.

Then the vet got a pair of scissors and snipped a bit of fur off Jim's leg. I wish she hadn't done that, but she had to find a vein to inject the morphine into. Jim must have been weak because she just put her head down on her paws and went to sleep. I stroked her once more and the vet then showed us out the side door.

I spent the rest of the day crying and sat up most of the night thinking and crying. I managed to get through the next day at school but had a good cry at home that evening. I thought that maybe by then I would've cried enough, but I now know that you can't cry too much. It's been a month since she died and sometimes I have a good cry. I think about her a lot. Jimbo was a lovely cat and I realize I was lucky to have owned her. I hope if we get another cat I will be as proud of her as I was of Jimbo.

HATTIE CASTELBERG   AGE 11   BRENTFORD, MIDDLESEX

Snowy

My family have a white rabbit called Snowy, which we found in our garden in December 1990. We thought it was a domestic rabbit, so we started putting out food for it. After it had been outside in our garden for about a month, we started to get worried about it as it was extremely cold and snowy outside. So we decided to see if we could find anyone in our village who had lost a rabbit.

We asked about and found someone who had let loose two rabbits just because they didn't want them anymore. The rabbit we had was one of them. The man pleaded with us to keep the rabbit and not to tell his two boys about it. We of course said we would. He then gave us his hutch, some hay and food and we took it home. There was already fresh hay and newspaper in the hutch so we put in fresh food and water. It didn't really take long for the rabbit to jump into his hutch, and when he was in he gobbled up his food. We placed his hutch in our porch and decided to call him Snowy because we found him in the snow.

The next day we took him to our vet because one of his ears was drooping. The vet said he had been attacked by an animal while he had been outside. The vet said his ear would soon heal and we were to feed him up as he was very thin. A few weeks later a piece of ear fell off one of his ears so we took him back to the vet. Luckily it was only frost-bite that would soon heal. He said it might happen to his other ear but it didn't.

Snowy is happy and well living in his hutch. We think it was cruel of the people to let him loose but were glad we found him and took him in.

NAOMI LOXHAM   AGE 10   BRIDGE OF WEIR,
RENFREWSHIRE

14

HORSES AND DONKEYS MATTER TOO

Horses Matter

In 1992 horses and ponies from all around the British Isles are going to be sold and transported to the continent for slaughter. Since the late 1960s there has been a law that stopped it, but now because of the EEC it will all be forgotten. The journey over to the continent is a dangerous and most uncomfortable one, that can last up to anything like seventeen hours. The transport is normally without straw or wood shavings, so the horses have to stand on metal. Horses do not like going to the loo with no covering on the floor,

so they could be waiting for a long time. When
travelling, injuries occur very easily and can
bleed for ages until they reach their
destination. Some will die during the journey.
When they arrive they do get inspected by a
vet but she or he may only check eyes and
ears. The horses rest for two days and then
are auctioned. Their death is a quick one and
is done by a shot through the head but some
have to stand in pens next to dead carcasses.

My friends and I are in the Pony Club and
we are desperate for the trade to stop. Horses
don't deserve to be treated like they are; they
never do anything to hurt us, but look how we
treat them in return. Horses are friends that
you love and have a lot of fun with. A super
partnership grows and you don't want anything
to spoil it. During holidays you go and
compete in competitions and the horses love
their lives. They do not want to be shot and
sold for meat, but they don't have a say. Really
only the dealers want them for meat; everyone
else loves them. Horses are our friends and we
don't want them to go.

Campaigns are trying to get a limit of 8
hours for the longest journey, but as the money
for horses is so high they don't think Brussels
will agree to it. People are also sending letters
to MPs telling them to stop the trade but
unless more people stand up and make a fuss
nothing will happen. The advert the RSPCA
did in the newspaper with the horse on a meat
hook was banned, saying it was too violent,

but nothing anybody does could be too much until the trade is stopped. The more fuss the better, but for now it happens in the continent and in 1992 will happen with horses and ponies from all around Britain.

OONAGH CARNWATH   AGE 12   SHEPRETH, HERTS.

The Rescue!

BANG! The horse-box doors slammed shut and darkness surrounded me. What was happening? There had been many long conversations, and I had heard my name, Borodin, mentioned several times. Now this. Where was I going? The engine started and the bumpy journey began. It seemed to go on forever, but at last the jolting stopped and the doors opened. Outside was a place that I had never seen before. Pens of horses were everywhere; the animals were frightened and scared, some of them were injured, their eyes rolling.

‘Right, this is the young shire-horse that’s going for slaughter,’ I heard someone say. ‘Put him over there with that lot.’ I was led out of my box, but before I got to the pen I heard a new voice.

‘Excuse me, is this Borodin, the young shire we heard about?’

‘I think so, yeah.’

‘Well, we’re from Horses And Ponies Protection Association and I believe Borodin will be coming with us. We have the papers.'

I was put into a new box and driven away.
When the doors were opened I looked on to a
long stretch of grass with donkeys standing
here and there.

'You'll be safe now Borodin,' said the voice
as I was pushed out into my field.

So began my new life at Capel Manor, one
of three sanctuaries owned by HAPPA for
horses and donkeys rescued from unhappy
homes or slaughter houses like me. I will stay
here for the rest of my life, so my story really
does have a 'HAPPA' ending!

LOUISA FIELDING   AGE 11   LYMINGTON, HANTS.

Adopting Donkeys

It was only a year ago now when I adopted a
donkey called Snowy, and I'm glad I did now.
The idea came when I went on holiday to the
Isle of Wight and met my pen-pal Zoë. We
always write to each other and in one of her
letters she told me she had adopted a donkey
and had sent me some details of how to adopt.
You pay £10 a year and they always write and
tell you how your donkey is. So I sent back
the adoption slip and sent the £10 for the first
year which is shared out between all the
donkeys to buy their food. I think the donkey
sanctuary is a good idea. They try to save
donkeys from being sold for dog food. The
Isle of Wight's donkey sanctuary costs so little,

but means so much. And why did I adopt Snowy? Because I think all animals matter and have a right to live.

LAURA-LEE HEUGH   AGE 10   IPSWICH, SUFFOLK

This donkey is called Blackie Star.
He is at a donkey sanctuary in Devon.
He is my favourite donkey there.
He was cruelly treated but was rescued by the
   sanctuary.
People should be kind to donkeys.
They are lovely animals.

AMY COLLINS   AGE 7   BATH, SOMERSET

The Pony's Ordeal

I walk through the street on my way to the
   fair,
don't know what to expect, don't know what is
   there.
I drew back in alarm for what I could see –
was a picture of horror, I was tempted to flee.
A small shabby pony tied and scared,
he had obviously been beaten extremely hard.
His eyelids were heavy, his head hung down,
his owner stood by with a stern-looking frown.
The pony tried to turn and run,
the man lifted his stick, he thought this was
   fun.
The stick came down with an awful crack,
leaving a scar red-raw on his back.
He was led into the ring after a terrifying wait
where the poor little pony was reaching his
   fate.
Would anyone buy him? Does anyone care?
He really wishes that he wasn't there.
But a kind looking girl patted his head,
'Dad, I want this one,' the little girl said.
He felt the love, the warmth as well,
she was to be his owner, the pony could tell.
But this pony was lucky unlike many more,
for the others just spare at least a thought.
Before buying a horse make sure you're aware
that *animals matter* and that you should care!

JULIETTE FEIRN   AGE 14   ATTLEBOROUGH, NORFOLK

ANSWERS TO PUZZLES

CONSERVATION BOX

Across

1. Mink   4. Hunt   6. Falcon   7. Badger
8. Dolphin   10. Puffin   11. Whale   14. Shark
15. Tiger   16. Dodo   18. Ivory
19. Pollution

Down

2. Kingfisher   3. Acid rain   5. Tern
7. Blubber   9. Bat   12. Extinct   13. Elephant
17. Owl

ANIMAL PUZZLES

1. Wordsearch

Unused letters spell: ZEBRA

2. Animal Riddle
   PANDA

'WHAT AM I?'
An Octopus

MONKEYS – WE NEED THEM!

PAWS AND CLAWS
1. Oyster-catcher 2. Otter 3. Cow 4. Mouse
5. Badger 6. Rabbit 7. Squirrel 8. Cat
9. Deer 10. Fox 11. Horse

SNAIL SPIRAL
1. Orang-outang 2. Gnat 3. Terrapin
4. Newt 5. Toucan 6. Narwhal
7. Lapwing 8. Gazelle 9. Elephant

BIRD-SEARCH

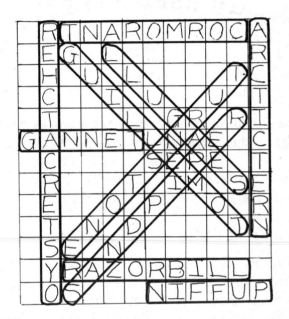

RAIN FOREST WORDSEARCH

M	H	U	M	M	I	N	G	B	I	R	D	Y
O	S	T	O	R	T	O	I	S	E	Z	H	A
N	R	O	F	J	P	D	H	M	B	G	T	N
K	Z	U	U	C	I	A	U	A	H	S	O	T
E	A	C	R	Y	X	L	R	P	E	O	L	E
Y	C	A	P	J	C	E	K	R	M	T	S	A
S	W	N	G	A	K	M	B	T	O	B	K	T
M	A	C	A	W	S	U	S	P	M	T	U	E
N	B	U	T	T	E	R	F	L	Y	E	S	R
F	O	P	L	E	D	T	U	R	T	L	E	S

THE RSPB SAYS . . .

The Royal Society for the Protection of Birds,
The Lodge, Sandy, Bedfordshire SG19 2DL

Help us protect puffins and we'll send you a
FREE FULL-COLOUR POSTER!

Wonderful Puffins

Puffins are the clowns of the sea cliffs. Their
multicoloured bills, rolling walk and laughing
calls make them wonderful birds.

Puffin colonies are great places to visit, but
they're often hard to get to – many are on
offshore islands. The birds spend the autumn
and winter far out to sea and return to nest in
April or May. Their one egg is laid in a burrow
on the cliff-top and both parents feed the young.
The young puffin has to make its own way out
of the burrow, down the cliffs, and out to sea.

Threatened

Like many creatures in our modern world,
puffins are threatened by people. Some perish
in oil-slicks, some die in fishing nets, and many
have starved in Shetland because of a decline
in the small fish (called sand-eels) that they eat.

Animals Matter

The Royal Society for the Protection of Birds believes birds and other animals really do matter. We want a healthy environment that is good for birds and other wildlife, and good for people, too.

How can you help?

By buying this book you are already helping, because the royalties from this book will help the RSPB save birds' lives. To say 'thank you', we will send you a free poster if you write to us.

Send your name, address (and postcode) and your age to Animals Matter, RSPB, Department N3012, The Lodge, Sandy, Bedfordshire SG19 2DL. When we send you your free poster, we'll also send you details of how you can join the world's biggest club for young people interested in birds and other wildlife – the Young Ornithologists' Club!

PUFFIN BY MIKE LANGMAN

PUFFINS BY ROB HUME

Bempton Cliffs
R.A. Hume 1979

A Note from the Editor

Many of the competition entries consisted of text *and* illustrations. Unfortunately, we have been unable to reproduce some of the colour illustrations, including the prizewinners on pages 47 and 79. Apologies to these contributors.